Edexcel GCSE

Digital
Communication

Student Book

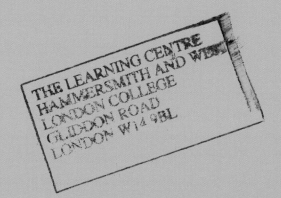

Lynn Burton
Mandy Esseen
Jonathan Morgan
Racheal Smith
Samantha Williams
Consultant: Racheal Smith

A PEARSON COMPANY

Contents

Introduction

Welcome to Edexcel GCSE Digital Communication. I'm really pleased to introduce you to this new and exciting qualification which will help you to analyse and use texts that you might not have chance to study elsewhere. I believe that the course will help you with the work you will complete in your English lessons, as well as making you literate in the 21st century.

The rapid development of technology over the last few decades has transformed the way that we communicate with each other, how we access information and how we are entertained. You now need to be skilled and confident in reading, assessing and creating different types of digital texts, as well as being confident with more traditional printed texts.

This course is designed to improve the skills that you already use on a daily basis, for example when you use the internet, watch a film or listen to a podcast. It will also help equip you for the world of work, as most jobs now need at least some level of knowledge and skill with digital texts.

During this course you will be asked to read critically many digital texts such as film, other moving image texts, websites and podcasts. As well as asking you to study these text, we give you the opportunity to be creative and produce your own digital texts for a particular audience and purpose. This could mean producing your own website or creating your own film!

I will be working hard with the team from Edexcel to help you do your best with this course. I hope you enjoy working through the materials in this book and it supports you to do the best you can do.

I look forward to reading and experiencing your work.

Racheal Smith

Senior Examiner for GCSE Digital Communication and Head of English at Bishop Fox's School.

The course

GCSE Digital Communication introduces you to English through the study and production of digital texts. A digital text is any text that can be stored and displayed in some way using computer technology.

Here is an overview of what the course covers:

Unit 1: Critical Reading of Moving Image Texts

Have you ever wondered how a film captures the imagination of an audience? What does a film-maker do to make you sad or scared or happy? In this unit you will explore the techniques used by film-makers including sound, lighting, camera angles and choices of set and direction. You will apply this knowledge to two films of the same genre (type), looking closely at specific examples and considering the overall intended effect.

Unit 2: Developing Skills in Critical Reading

You are probably already an expert with social networking websites such as Facebook, MySpace and Twitter. However, to be truly digitally literate you need the skills to analyse all types of digital texts. This means considering the choices made by the writer, the intended purpose of the text, and its strengths and weaknesses.

This unit builds on what you already know and gives you the language to respond to texts with insight and skill.

Unit 3: Creating a Digital Text

In this unit you can apply what you have learned in Units 1 and 2 about techniques and impact. You will be given a brief and your task will be to produce a digital text to fulfil the brief. It could be creating a website, digital video or podcast. You will be expected to produce detailed plans, evidence of research and an evaluation along with your final digital text.

This is an exciting unit that gives you the opportunity to show what you can do by thinking about everything it takes to make a professional and interesting digital text.

The assessment

Here is an overview of how you will be assessed in each unit:

Unit 1 Critical Reading of Moving Image Texts

This is a controlled assessment unit worth 20% of the GCSE.

The assessment asks you to focus on a specific film genre, such as science fiction or comedy, and a particular film from within this genre. There will be two genres, each with a choice of two tasks. You will choose one genre and respond to one task. The task is in three parts:

- **Section A:** You will consider what the audience learns about named characters from a selected scene in the film you have studied.
- **Section B:** You will choose and analyse another short extract from the film in relation to how the mood and atmosphere are created.
- **Section C:** You will explore how the film you have studied challenges or conforms to its genre, drawing on at least one other moving image text from that genre.

Unit 2 Developing Skills in Critical Reading

This is an examination unit worth 40% of the GCSE.

You will study six pre-released digital texts such as websites (which can include podcasts, forums, social networks, blogs), moving image, e-mail and mobile communication. You will be asked questions on two unseen texts and one on the pre-released texts. The examination is in two sections:

- **Section A:** You will read and critique two unseen digital texts, exploring the audience, purpose, meaning, impact and register. You may also be asked to write about the components of digital texts, compare digital texts and respond to stimulus material.
- **Section B:** You will carry out a critical reading of one of the pre-released digital texts and will be asked questions about the convention, form, mode and text type.

Unit 3 Creating a Digital Text

This is a controlled assessment unit worth 40% of the GCSE.

You will produce a digital text of your choice, such as a podcast, moving image or website, which responds to a set brief. The task is in three parts:

- **Section A:** You will write a proposal for your own text, showing how it will meet the brief you have been given.
- **Section B:** You will create and edit the content of your digital text, ensuring that it meets the brief you have been given.
- **Section C:** You will explain the reasons for the choices you made when creating your digital text, drawing on feedback that you have had from others.

About this book

This student book has been designed to help you to learn and develop the knowledge and skills you need to have an enjoyable and successful experience in GCSE Digital Communication. It is divided into three units, with each unit broken down further into chapters. Here are some of the key features that make this book as user-friendly as possible:

Objectives at the beginning of each chapter provide a clear overview of what you will learn.

Key Terms are highlighted in the text and are defined in margin boxes.

Additional digital resources are available on the **companion website**.

Engaging **activities** help you develop the skills you need.

ResultsPlus features give guidance on how to achieve better results.

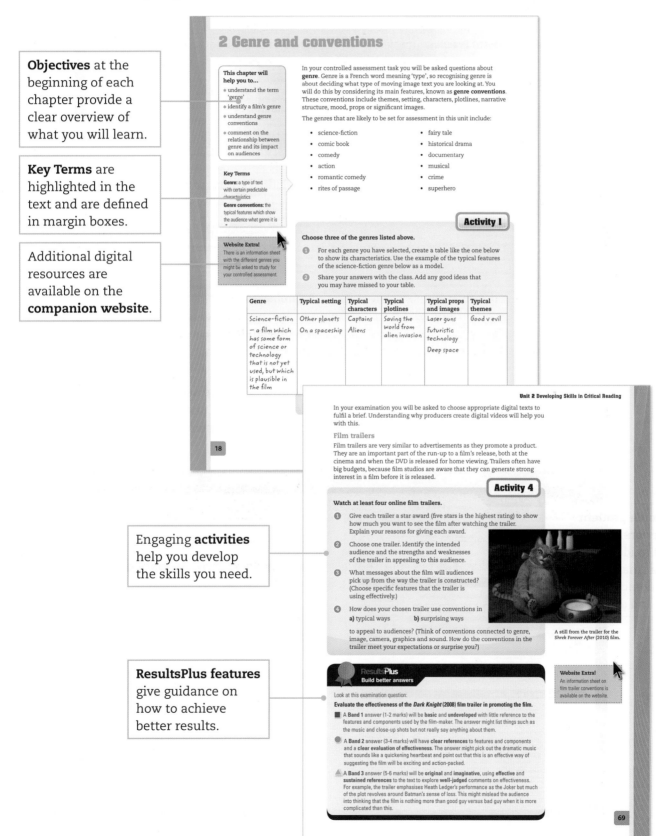

2 Genre and conventions

This chapter will help you to...
- understand the term 'genre'
- identify a film's genre
- understand genre conventions
- comment on the relationship between genre and its impact on audiences

Key Terms

Genre: a type of text with certain predictable characteristics

Genre conventions: the typical features which show the audience what genre it is

Website Extra!
There is an information sheet with the different genres you might be asked to study for your controlled assessment.

In your controlled assessment task you will be asked questions about **genre**. Genre is a French word meaning 'type', so recognising genre is about deciding what type of moving image text you are looking at. You will do this by considering its main features, known as **genre conventions**. These conventions include themes, setting, characters, plotlines, narrative structure, mood, props or significant images.

The genres that are likely to be set for assessment in this unit include:

- science-fiction
- comic book
- comedy
- action
- romantic comedy
- rites of passage
- fairy tale
- historical drama
- documentary
- musical
- crime
- superhero

Activity 1

Choose three of the genres listed above.

1. For each genre you have selected, create a table like the one below to show its characteristics. Use the example of the typical features of the science-fiction genre below as a model.

2. Share your answers with the class. Add any good ideas that you may have missed to your table.

Genre	Typical setting	Typical characters	Typical plotlines	Typical props and images	Typical themes
Science-fiction – a film which has some form of science or technology that is not yet used, but which is plausible in the film	Other planets On a spaceship	Captains Aliens	Saving the world from alien invasion	Laser guns Futuristic technology Deep space	Good v evil

18

In your examination you will be asked to choose appropriate digital texts to fulfil a brief. Understanding why producers create digital videos will help you with this.

Film trailers

Film trailers are very similar to advertisements as they promote a product. They are an important part of the run-up to a film's release, both at the cinema and when the DVD is released for home viewing. Trailers often have big budgets, because film studios are aware that they can generate strong interest in a film before it is released.

Activity 4

Watch at least four online film trailers.

1. Give each trailer a star award (five stars is the highest rating) to show how much you want to see the film after watching the trailer. Explain your reasons for giving each award.

2. Choose one trailer. Identify the intended audience and the strengths and weaknesses of the trailer in appealing to this audience.

3. What messages about the film will audiences pick up from the way the trailer is constructed? (Choose specific features that the trailer is using effectively.)

4. How does your chosen trailer use conventions in
   a) typical ways   b) surprising ways

   to appeal to audiences? (Think of conventions connected to genre, image, camera, graphics and sound. How do the conventions in the trailer meet your expectations or surprise you?)

A still from the trailer for the *Shrek Forever After* (2010) film.

ResultsPlus
Build better answers

Look at this examination question:
Evaluate the effectiveness of the *Dark Knight* (2008) film trailer in promoting the film.

- A **Band 1** answer (1-2 marks) will be **basic** and **undeveloped** with little reference to the features and components used by the film-maker. The answer might list things such as the music and close-up shots but not really say anything about them.

- A **Band 2** answer (3-4 marks) will have **clear references** to features and components and a **clear evaluation of effectiveness**. The answer might pick out the dramatic music that sounds like a quickening heartbeat and point out that this is an effective way of suggesting the film will be exciting and action-packed.

- A **Band 3** answer (5-6 marks) will be **original** and **imaginative**, using **effective** and **sustained references** to the text to explore **well-judged** comments on effectiveness. For example, the trailer emphasises Heath Ledger's performance as the Joker but much of the plot revolves around Batman's sense of loss. This might mislead the audience into thinking that the film is nothing more than good guy versus bad guy when it is more complicated than this.

Website Extra!
An information sheet on film trailer conventions is available on the website.

69

At the end of each unit there is a **Controlled Assessment Practice** or **Examination Practice** section. This explains how you will be assessed and what you are being assessed on, and gives you tips on how to succeed. It also has sample controlled assessment or examination papers so you can see what these will look like.

Detailed **information about your assessment** will help you understand what you need to do to succeed.

Sample **controlled assessment tasks** and **examination papers**, with detailed comments from the examiner, will help you prepare for the assessment.

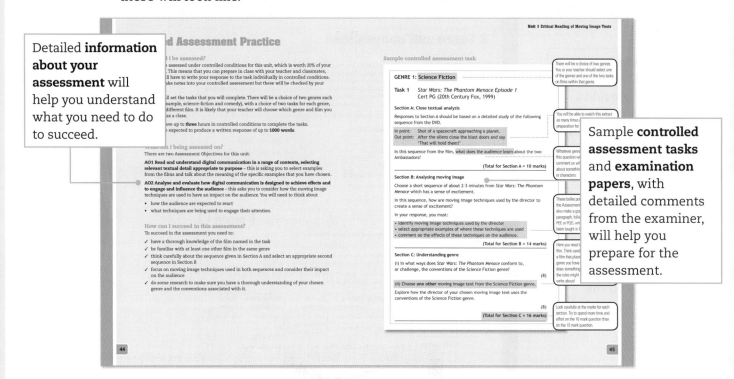

Each Controlled Assessment Practice or Examination Practice section is followed by **ResultsPlus Maximise Your Marks**. These pages show you sample student answers at different grades to some controlled assessment tasks and examination questions.

Sample student answers enable you to identify what makes the difference between a C and an A grade.

Examiner comments guide you through the student answers and summarise the key differences between the grades.

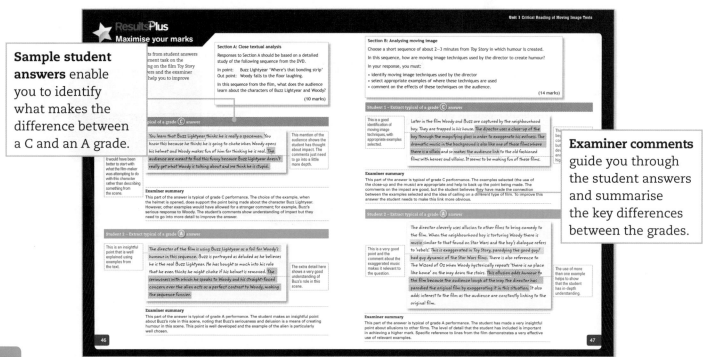

Results**Plus**

ResultsPlus features combine expert advice and guidance from examiners to show you how to achieve better results.

Results Plus
Build better answers

Look at this part of a controlled assessment task:

In what ways does *Shrek* (2001) use, or challenge, the conventions of the comedy genre?

■ A **Band 1** answer (1–3 marks) might tell the story – that Shrek is an ogre and he has a friend that is a donkey – and comment that the film is a comedy, which shows **limited understanding** of the genre conventions.

● A **Band 2** answer (4–5 marks) will show **sound understanding** of the features of the film *Shrek* that make it a comedy. For example, mentioning that the partnership of Shrek and the donkey is like a classic comedy duo where there is a serious man and a character that makes fun of this.

▲ A **Band 3** answer (6–8 marks) will develop this to show **perceptive understanding** of the features of genre. For example, the response might include the fact that the film draws on the features of fantasy and fairy tale by using ogres and talking animals. With a cartoon form, this leads the audience to believe that this is less a comedy and more a fantastical children's film.

Build better answers features give you an exam-style question or part of a controlled assessment task and help you to understand the mark scheme against which you will be assessed. These features show what you need to do in your response to the task to achieve the marks in each band.

Results Plus
Self assessment

Check your answer **to question 2** in **Activity 9**. Have you:
• described specific techniques used in the film?
• considered their effects on the audience?

Self assessment features help you to check your answers to activities to make sure you have demonstrated the skills you will need to show in your assessment.

Results Plus
Controlled assessment tip

▲ When selecting the second film for your controlled assessment choose a film that does something slightly different with the genre. This will give you something different and interesting to explore.

Exam tip and **Controlled assessment tip** features provide examiner advice and guidance to help improve your results.

Watch out features warn you about common mistakes that examiners frequently see students make. Make sure you don't repeat them!

Results Plus
Watch out

■ Just telling the story of a film will get you very few marks. You need to explore the techniques used by the film-maker to help them tell the story. One of these techniques is narrative structure.

Companion website

Additional digital resources are available on the Digital Communication companion website. The website address is http://www.contentextra.com/ digitalcomm. You will need a user name and password to access the website and these can be found on page 151. The **Website extra!** boxes throughout the student book show you when extra materials are available to help you.

Turn to page 151 to find out your **user name** and **password**.

Resources are grouped by unit for **easy navigation**.

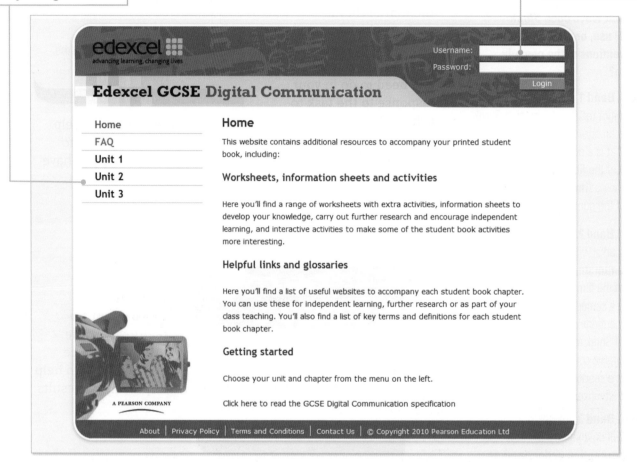

Website Extra!

The **Website Extra!** boxes indicate when additional resources are available on the website.

The digital resources available on the companion website include:

- **interactive activities**
- **worksheets** – additional activities and copies of all the tables for you to fill in for activities throughout the student book
- **glossaries** – chapter-by-chapter glossaries
- **information sheets** – additional information to help build on your knowledge
- **weblinks** – to all the websites, videos and podcasts in the student book.

Interactive activities

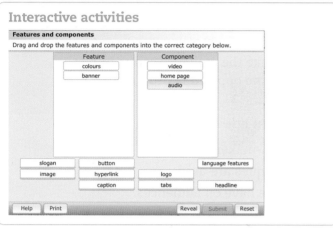

Worksheets

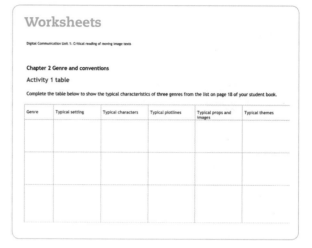

Information sheets

Digital Communication Unit 3: Creating digital text

Chapter 4 Capturing components

Camera shots and camera angles

Example	Camera shot/angle	Description
	Close up	The close up focuses just on the head and shoulders of the person in the shot. We can see the detail of the subject's facial expressions when a close up is used.
	Extreme close up	In an extreme close up one part of the subject or object completely fills the shot, e.g. an image of an eye rather than the whole of the subject's face.
	Over the shoulder	In this shot the subject is shown over the shoulder of another subject.
	Three shot	This includes three subjects in the shot.

Glossaries

Chapter 2 Genre and conventions

cross-genre	when at least two genres are brought together combining the conventions of both genres; for example, the superhero movie combines the genres of superhero comics and action films
genre	a type of media text with certain predictable characteristics
genre conventions	the typical features in a film which show the audience what genre it is

© Pearson Education 2010

Weblinks

Unit 1 Critical reading of moving image texts

Have you ever wondered how a film captures the imagination of an audience? How does a film-maker make the audience sad or happy? Unit 1 is all about film and gives you the opportunity to consider these questions and many more.

In this student book unit you will learn how to:

• identify the techniques used by film-makers

• consider how and why these techniques are used

• explore the impact these techniques have on audiences.

Your assessment

Unit 1 is a controlled assessment unit, in which you will complete one task. Your task will focus on a specific film genre, such as science fiction or comedy, and on a particular film within this genre.

Following your preparation time:

• you will have **three hours** to complete the task

• you can write up to **1000 words** in your response.

The task is in three parts:

Section A: Close textual analysis – this question asks you to explain what the audience learns about named characters from a selected scene in the film you have studied.

Section B: Analysing moving image – this question asks you to choose and analyse another short extract from the film in relation to the theme (for example, how the film-maker has created the mood and atmosphere).

Section C: Understanding genre – this question asks you to explore how the film you have studied challenges or conforms to its genre, and then asks you to analyse how another film of your choice relates to the same genre.

Assessment Objectives

Your Unit 1 controlled assessment response will be marked using these Assessment Objectives:

AO1 Read and understand digital communication in a range of contexts, selecting relevant textual detail appropriate to purpose.

AO2 Analyse and evaluate how digital communication is designed to achieve effects and to engage and influence the audience/reader.

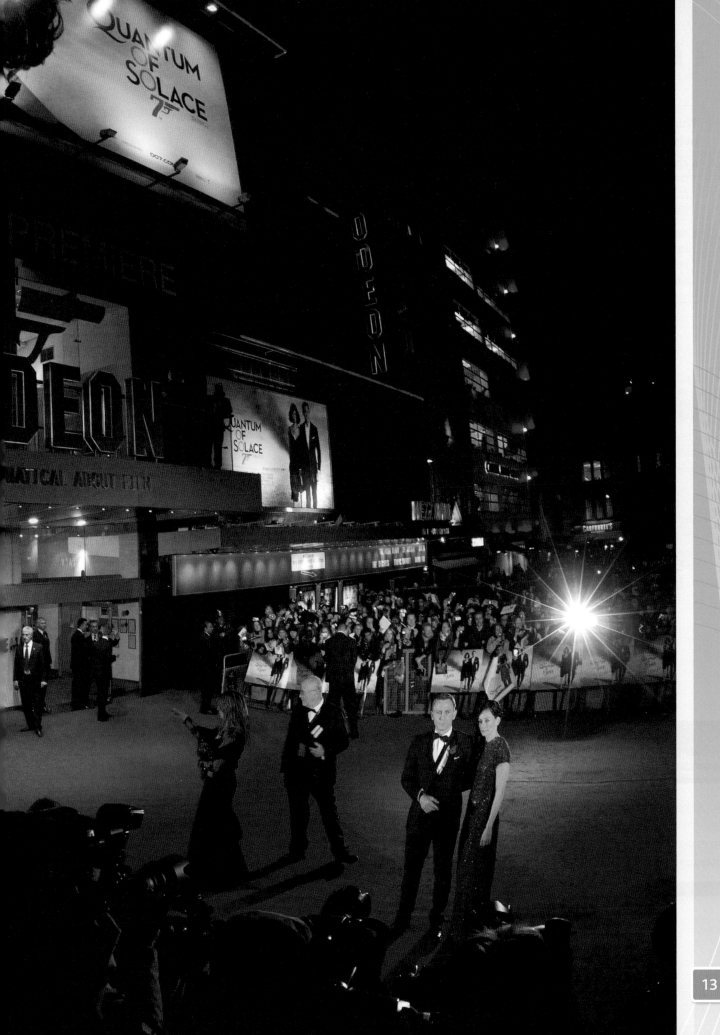

1 Audience, purpose and impact

This chapter will help you to...

* consider the intended impact of a moving image text on the audience

* analyse how this impact has been achieved by the film-maker

Website Extra!

There is a checklist for reading a text on the website. You can refer to this to see how you can apply the reading skills you use when exploring a traditional literary/non-literary text to 'reading' a moving image.

Results Plus
Controlled assessment tip

Remember to use the questions in this flow chart in preparation for your controlled assessment task.

In your controlled assessment task it is important to consider the audience and intended impact on that audience when answering questions about the film you have studied.

When analysing a moving image text you need to use the same approach and skills that you use when analysing a paper text, such as a newspaper article. For all texts, you will need to consider the following:

	Definition	Examples
Purpose	The aim of the text	To entertain/engage/amuse To inspire/raise awareness of an issue To shock/disturb/ridicule
Audience	Who the text is aimed at	Young teenagers Couples
Techniques	How the aim is achieved	Use of editing devices and techniques in a film
Intended impact	How the audience is expected to respond	To become more aware of an issue To be entertained To feel anger/guilt/empathy

In your controlled assessment you will need to consider the intended impact on the audience of the film you are studying. You will also need to consider whether you feel this impact/effect has been achieved by the film-maker. This may seem difficult if you are not the intended audience, but you will need to imagine how someone else would react to the film.

To consider the intended impact of the moving image text on the audience, ask yourself these questions:

What is the purpose of the text?

Who is the target audience, and what are their interests and needs?

How would the target audience respond to this text?

Is this response what the film-maker intended?

Gender and age

Film-makers will usually have a clear idea about the gender and age of their intended audience. You can often identify a film as targeting a gender by the subject matter, themes or values at its heart. For example, complex emotional dramas which consider human reactions to moral dilemmas, such as *My Sister's Keeper* (2009), are more likely to be enjoyed by female audiences. On the other hand, slapstick comedies, such as the *Police Academy* films (1984–94), are more popular with male audiences.

Film-makers will also consider the age of the intended audience to ensure they make choices that appeal to, and are suitable for, that age range.

My Sister's Keeper is an emotional drama which is more likely to appeal to a female audience.

A slapstick comedy such as *Police Academy* is more likely to appeal to a male audience.

Activity 1

Crime films are often targeted at men. They usually feature male detectives and criminals, whose intelligence and strength we learn about in great detail. They also tend to focus on the crime investigation process, often with lots of weapons and/or forensic science.

1. If you wanted to make a crime film targeted at women, what elements might you want to change?

2. Think about your controlled assessment film – does it target specific audiences by gender? How does the film-maker appeal to this audience?

Look at the following descriptions of audiences by age band.

3. Match each audience to the age band it belongs to.

Under 10s

This group enjoy high-budget films with lots of action, e.g. *The Matrix* (1999).

Young teenagers, aged 12–14

This group cannot go to the cinema alone so films have to appeal to parents too, e.g. the *Toy Story* (1995–2010) films.

Older teenagers, aged 15–20

In this group girls and boys are experiencing a search for identity, so films are often gender-specific, e.g. *Twilight* (2008) or *Transformers* (2007).

Adults, aged 21–45

This group often visit the cinema in couples or rent/buy films to watch at home. Films often target couples and try to make the film appealing by employing famous stars or directors, e.g. *The Pursuit of Happyness* (2006).

Sometimes, even if a film-maker has carefully placed elements in a film to appeal to a particular audience, another audience can also enjoy it. For example, *The Full Monty* (1997) was a low-budget British comedy aimed at older, mainly female audiences, but it also gained huge popularity with younger audiences of both sexes who enjoyed the soundtrack, themes and humour.

Emotions and ideas

It is important to consider the emotions and ideas that the film-maker intended the audience to have in reaction to the film.

In your controlled assessment task you will need to consider the intended impact on the audience and analyse how this impact is achieved.

Activity 2

Select three films you know well. You might want to investigate them on IMDb (The Internet Movie Database).

1. What emotions are the audience meant to feel when watching each film?

2. What ideas is the film-maker asking the audience to explore in each film?

Activity 3

Watch the opening of Baz Luhrmann's *Romeo + Juliet* (1996).

1. How does the film-maker try to entertain a teenage audience who might be expecting an 'old-fashioned and hard to understand' Shakespeare film? Make notes on the following aspects of the first ten minutes:

   • the unusual modern setting

   • the use of television news bulletins

   • the use of onscreen text to make the characters look like actors in a TV show

   • the camerawork – fast-paced and exciting shots

   • the modern music.

Activity 4

1. Choose a film from your controlled assessment focus genre and discuss how the audience might respond to it.

2. Explain how the film-maker has tried to catch the audience's attention. Consider the use of camerawork, music, the interaction and dialogue between characters and the use of famous stars.

Preparing for your controlled assesment

In your controlled assessment task you will need to consider the audience, purpose and intended impact on the audience. To prepare for this question you should:

• Explore the intended audience groups of your chosen film and what their needs might be in choosing to watch the film.

• Consider the messages for the audience in your chosen film. This will help you to identify key scenes that are deliberately created to be tense, exciting, sad, funny, etc.

• Analyse your chosen film from the viewpoint of different audience groups – for example, how might a male viewer respond differently from a female viewer to the film?

• Watch key scenes from your film and practise commenting on the mood and atmosphere created by the director.

2 Genre and conventions

This chapter will help you to...

* understand the term 'genre'
* identify a film's genre
* understand genre conventions
* comment on the relationship between genre and its impact on audiences

Key Terms

Genre: a type of text with certain predictable characteristics

Genre conventions: the typical features which show the audience what genre it is

Website Extra!

There is an information sheet with the different genres you might be asked to study for your controlled assessment.

In your controlled assessment task you will be asked questions about **genre**. Genre is a French word meaning 'type', so recognising genre is about deciding what type of moving image text you are looking at. You will do this by considering its main features, known as **genre conventions**. These conventions include themes, setting, characters, plotlines, narrative structure, mood, props or significant images.

The genres that are likely to be set for assessment in this unit include:

* science-fiction
* comic book
* comedy
* action
* romantic comedy
* rites of passage
* fairy tale
* historical drama
* documentary
* musical
* crime
* superhero

Activity 1

Choose three of the genres listed above.

1. For each genre you have selected, create a table like the one below to show its characteristics. Use the example of the typical features of the science-fiction genre below as a model.

2. Share your answers with the class. Add any good ideas that you may have missed to your table.

Genre	Typical setting	Typical characters	Typical plotlines	Typical props and images	Typical themes
Science-fiction — a film which has some form of science or technology that is not yet used, but which is plausible in the film	Other planets On a spaceship	Captains Aliens	Saving the world from alien invasion	Laser guns Futuristic technology Deep space	Good v evil

You can often tell from watching just a few seconds of a film or film trailer what genre that film belongs to. What film genre do the words 'explosions' and 'car chases' suggest?

You probably thought 'action' before you even read the second word!

Activity 2

Look closely at the two film posters below.

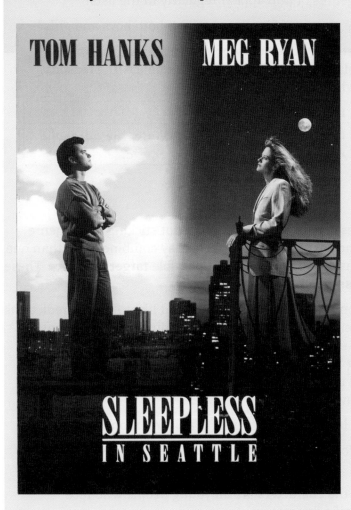
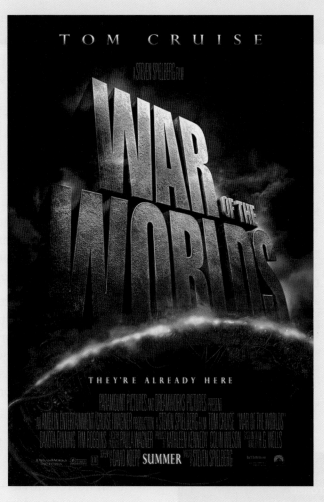

1. Identify the genre of each film.

2. What are the key genre conventions used in the posters that helped you decide what genre each film belongs to?

3. What would audiences expect to experience in each of the genres represented by these posters?

Film-makers rely on people's ability to recognise genre when they promote new films to create interest, expectation and anticipation.

Activity 3

1. Choose your two favourite films and make brief notes about why you like them.

2. Working as a class, combine your chosen films into a list. Look closely at the class choices.

   a) Do the same genres of film appear regularly in the lists?

   b) Were the same genres of film popular with both boys and girls?

3. Copy and complete the table below by listing the genres from the class list and explaining the impact on the audience (the reasons people gave for why they liked the films).

Film genre	Impact on the audience
Action film	Excitement, the thrill of a chase, the adrenalin rush of escaping from danger, etc.

Key Terms

Target audience: a group of people at whom a moving image text is aimed

Cross-genres: when at least two genres are brought together combining the conventions of both genres; for example, the superhero movie combines the genres of superhero comics and action films

ResultsPlus
Controlled assessment tip

⚠ When selecting the second film for your controlled assessment try to choose a film that does something slightly different with the genre. This will give you something different and interesting to explore.

Challenging genre

Film-makers sometimes surprise an audience by not sticking to the genre conventions the audience expects. Film-makers may combine more than one set of genre conventions to attract the widest possible **target audience**. These films are known as **cross-genres**.

Audiences enjoy the complexity of cross-genres, and like to make predictions about plot and characters based on their understanding of the different genre conventions. For example, *Cloverfield* (2008), which revolves around a monster attack on New York and is shown from the perspective of a small group of people, seems to be aimed at fans of the action genre. However, it also uses the genre conventions of:

- science fiction – the largely unseen threat is an alien monster

- documentary – the footage is shot using a documentary-style hand-held camera

- teen horror movie – the characters are all young people who face unexpected and horrific danger.

Activity 4

Choose an example of a cross-genre film you have watched. For example, you could choose: *Men in Black* (1997), *Kung Fu Panda* (2008) or *The Parole Officer* (2002).

1. Identify the different genre conventions used in the film.

2. What impact does this mix of genre conventions have on the audience?

Sub-genres

One film genre that is popular with teenagers is comedy. Comedy films appeal to both sexes. The humour is often based on a plausible situation that is taken to extremes, frequently with embarrassing consequences.

Activity 5

1. Conduct a 'comedy film survey'. What are the most popular comedies in your class? Why do you think this is?

Within the comedy genre there are **sub-genres** that are based on different types of humour.

Examples of popular comedy sub-genres include:

- **Slapstick comedy** – this is one of the oldest sub-genres of comedy. Its main conventions include situations where characters fall, are tripped up, are injured (although not really hurt) or have exaggerated fights. A good example is in the 1984 film *Ghostbusters* when Slimer rushes straight through Bill Murray's character, knocking him to the floor and covering him with green 'goo'. A more classic example of slapstick comedy is *Laurel and Hardy*. Why do you think the audience finds it funny when people fall over or experience embarrassing situations?

- **Teenage comedy** – this sub-genre has become very popular with teenage audiences in the last twenty years, with films such as *Superbad* (2007). Its main conventions include situations that teenagers might relate to, such as relationships with parents and members of the opposite sex, school and the difficulties of becoming an adult. It could be said that teenage comedies are only successful if they reflect the situations that teenagers really face in life. Do you agree?

> **Key Terms**
>
> **Sub-genre:** a division of a genre. For example, romantic comedy is a sub-genre of the comedy genre

Superbad is an example of a teenage comedy.

Simon Pegg plays a police officer in *Hot Fuzz*, an example of a spoof comedy.

ResultsPlus
Build better answers

Look at this part of a controlled assessment task:

In what ways does *Shrek* (2001) use, or challenge, the conventions of the comedy genre?

■ A **Band 1** answer (1–3 marks) might tell the story – that Shrek is an ogre and he has a friend that is a donkey – and comment that the film is a comedy, which shows **limited understanding** of the genre conventions.

● A **Band 2** answer (4–5 marks) will show **sound understanding** of the features of the film *Shrek* that make it a comedy. For example, mentioning that the partnership of Shrek and the donkey is like a classic comedy duo where there is a serious man and a character that makes fun of this.

▲ A **Band 3** answer (6–8 marks) will develop this to show **perceptive understanding** of the features of genre. For example, the response might include the fact that the film draws on the features of fantasy and fairy tale by using ogres and talking animals. With a cartoon form, this leads the audience to believe that this is less a comedy and more a fantastical children's film.

- **Spoof** – a spoof is a comedy that takes the genre conventions of a type of film but makes gentle fun of them. A good example is *Hot Fuzz* (2007) which takes the crime/police genre and makes it funny by using over-the-top violence, ridiculously exaggerated villains and a 'straight man' (played by Simon Pegg) who does not see the funny side of situations. A good spoof requires its audience to have a good understanding of genre. Why?

- **Cross-genre comedy** – many comedy films have incorporated other genre conventions. *Rush Hour* (1998), for example, includes the conventions of an action film and a comedy, with an unlikely partnership between an American and a Hong Kong martial arts expert.

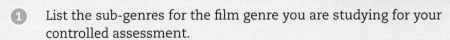

Activity 6

1. List the sub-genres for the film genre you are studying for your controlled assessment.

2. List three films for each of the sub-genres you identified in question 2.

Preparing for your controlled assessment

In your controlled assessment task you will be asked a question about how typical or challenging your film's genre is. To prepare for this question you should:

- Outline the conventions that are used in both your chosen film and another in the same genre that would help an audience identify to which genre they belong.

- Think about the audience's expectations of a film in the controlled assessment film genre you have studied. Does your chosen film meet those expectations, or does it offer something new and challenging?

- Analyse key scenes from your chosen film and one other film and decide which elements are the most typical for their genre, and which are unexpected, surprising or challenging in some way. This might be the setting, character, soundtrack, narrative timeline, use of camera, etc.

- Consider how your chosen film might make references to other films, texts or real-life events through intertextuality.

- Explore the extent to which your chosen film and comparison film might be sub-genres of a more general genre.

3 The language of moving image

In your controlled assessment task you will be asked a question about the moving image techniques used in the film you have studied. You will need to identify the techniques used by the film-maker to create meanings and messages that appeal to the audience and select appropriate examples where these techniques are used. You will also need to explain how these techniques impact on the audience.

The techniques covered in this chapter are:

- mise-en-scène
- camera techniques
- editing and transition
- special effects
- sound
- opening sequences

Mise-en-scène

Moving image texts are full of messages and meanings that will appeal to the audience.

The creation of every image, whether still or moving, involves planning and setting up. The careful arrangement of every element in an image to create a particular message, meaning and representation is called the **mise-en-scène**. The elements in a shot can include anything from the set, props, lighting and colour scheme to the subjects themselves and what they are wearing, how they are posed and their facial expressions.

This chapter will help you to...

* identify some of the techniques that create impact in films
* understand the importance of camerawork and editing in creating meaning
* make the connection between techniques used and impact on the viewer

Key Terms

Mise-en-scène: a French phrase which means 'put in shot'

Activity 1

Look at the two screen shots below.

1. List any differences between them that you can spot.

2. What impact do these differences have on the audience's understanding of the characters?

Website Extra!
Download the worksheet before completing Activity 2.

Activity 2

The best way to understand how mise-en-scène works is to try it yourself.

1. Imagine you are the director of a drama set in a school or college. You must set up an establishing shot of a character to communicate to the film's teenage audience that it is cool to be studious and work hard, as well as to be popular and trendy.

   An establishing shot is designed to give the viewer a sense of setting, genre and, quite often, character. Describe how you would create the mise-en scène. You will need to consider the following:

   - the setting
   - the subject
   - clothing and accessories for the subject
   - positioning and pose of the subject
   - positioning of any props
   - the angle of the shot

2. Now imagine that you are making a film focusing on the lives of a group of students aged 11–14. This is also your target audience. Your film centres on a student who hates school. Your task is to set up the shot that gives the audience their first look at this person. The messages you want to communicate about the person are that they hate school, are bored in their lesson and are desperate for the bell to go.

   Using only the elements you used in the first mise-en-scène, change the arrangement to create a different meaning. Remember to consider:

   - what changes you might make to the subject's clothing and accessories
   - how the positioning and pose of the subject might change
   - what might happen to the props
   - whether you should use a different camera angle.

3. Copy and complete the table below to record the changes that you have made.

Changes made between the two shots	Intended impact of the change

ResultsPlus
Controlled assessment tip

⚠ Avoid speaking too generally about a film. To get a good mark you need to look at small details and explain their effect on the audience.

Look at the still below from the film *Mean Girls* (2004). Read the notes around the image which show how you can analyse the mise-en-scène of a key moment from a film.

How are they represented?
All four characters are good looking. The three sitting down are wearing fashionable clothing and have their long hair loose. They all have their arms folded and have the same sort of food on their trays. The fourth character has plain clothes and her hair in a pony tail. She does not seem to conform to a 'girlie' image, unlike the girls sitting down.

What are their surroundings like?
There are other teenagers in the background and they are wearing more casual and less fashionable clothes than the three girls sitting down. There are lots of groups of friends sitting together and they all seem quite relaxed. The only spare seats are the ones in front of the three girls.

Who is in the shot?
A group of four teenagers are having lunch in an American high school cafeteria.

How are they positioned?
The four teenagers are divided into two groups. The three girls in the first group are sitting down with their arms crossed, looking at the fourth girl standing across from them. We know the three girls sitting down are friends because they are wearing similar clothes and look very similar. The fourth girl is an outsider as she is standing back from the table and looks unsure about whether she should sit down.

What meanings can the audience pick up from the mise-en-scène?
We can see that the girl standing up wants to join the three girls and they are deciding whether they should let her. The positioning of the three girls on one side of the table with empty chairs on the other makes a barrier and they look like a panel of judges. The girl standing up doesn't appear to fit in and the three girls appear to be making her uncomfortable.

Activity 3

Using what you have learned about how film-makers suggest meanings for their audiences, you are going to take a photograph of yourself or a friend as the star of an original new film.

1. Decide on the genre of the film.

2. List five bullet points that describe the character that your star will play. For example, for the star of a teenage drama you could include: *a strong personality, a unique sense of fashion.*

3. Now create a 'look' for your star that matches your description. Think carefully about the mise-en-scène of the photograph, so that the background is as appropriate as the costume and make-up. Set up the shot and take or ask someone to take the photograph. Make sure that your star's facial expression creates an impression of their personality.

ResultsPlus
Self assessment

Check your answer to **Activity 4**. Have you:

- selected small details from the scene that help to represent the type or stereotype of character (assessed in **Section A** of the controlled assessment task)?
- selected details from the scene that explore how the film-maker has created mood and atmosphere (assessed in **Section B** of the controlled assessment task)?
- considered how the details link to genre (assessed in **Section C** of the controlled assessment task)?

Activity 4

Choose a key scene from a film in the genre you are studying for your controlled assessment. Pause the film at a moment when something significant is happening and analyse the shot using the following questions:

1. Who is in the shot?

2. How are they positioned?

3. How are they represented through dress, props and facial expression?

4. What are their surroundings like?

5. What meanings can an audience pick up from this mise-en-scène?

Camera techniques

In order to analyse any moving image text, you need to identify how camera shots are used to communicate messages and meanings to audiences. Film-makers spend a lot of time organising and setting up every scene in a film. Cameras must be positioned in just the right way to capture on film exactly what the film-maker wants the audience to see, as this will affect how they respond to the text.

The table below describes some camera shots that you might be able to identify and comment on in your controlled assessment task. Examples of some of these camera shots (all film stills from *The Pursuit of Happyness*, 2006) are on page 28. Remember that it is important to analyse why the camera shots have been used and what impact they have on the audience.

Camera term	What term means/what impact it has
Establishing shot	The camera is set far back to show or to emphasise the setting or location that will be the backdrop of the action to come.
Long shot	The camera shows the subject in the context of the setting. This has the effect of showing us what the subject is doing and what is going on in the background.
Mid-shot	We see the subject from the waist up in order to have a better idea of their actions and expressions. This is often used to focus on the dialogue between two characters.
Close-up shot	This shot usually shows us the head and shoulders of the subject in order to focus attention on a character's reactions and emotions.
Extreme close-up	The camera shows us just one part of an object or subject, e.g. the eyes or knuckles, in order to draw attention to tiny details that add meaning for audiences.
Point of view shot	Sometimes the camera looks at a scene or a person from the viewpoint of another character.
Zoom	The camera focuses in on, or moves out from, a subject. It is usually used to emphasise a dramatic moment or reaction.
Travelling shot	The camera moves alongside the subject. This creates the effect of pace, as if we have joined the subject in the middle of the action.

Below are different camera shots from *The Pursuit of Happyness*.

Long shot

Mid-shot

Close-up shot

Activity 5

Look again at the two representations of teenagers that you created in Activity 2 in the section on mise-en-scène.

① What camera shots and angles did you choose?

② What effect do you think these choices will have on audiences?

Activity 6

Watch a key scene from a film of your choice three times – this could be a film from your controlled assessment focus genre.

① Make notes on the camera techniques that are used in this scene.

② What is the effect of these techniques on the audience?

Editing and transition

Moving image texts are made by placing sections of footage side by side into a sequence in order to make the narrative. Choosing and ordering footage, as well as creating title and end credit sequences, is the job of the editor. Editing techniques form an important part of the style and 'look' of a film.

It is important to understand how a film has been edited and why the film-maker has made these choices. Read the bullet points below which focus on the editing techniques used in the opening ten minutes of *Quantum of Solace* (2008). The bullet points analyse a section of the film by focusing on and interpreting the small details in a moving image text. The key terms are explained in the margin so remember to look at these.

- Bond films usually open with a **prologue**.

- This film opens with a **fade-in** to a fast travelling shot over water towards a coastline.

- The travelling shot **cuts** to a car chase through a tunnel, then cuts back to the travelling shot.

- The next cut is to an extreme close-up on the driver's eye and we may recognise him as James Bond (Daniel Craig).

- Suddenly the **pace** accelerates and follows the violent car chase using fast cut editing and close-up camerawork.

- The pace slows down as Bond pulls away, and the camera uses more long shots and establishing shots to give us clues that we are in Italy.

- A final close-up on Bond's face then cuts into the title sequence.

- The editing is fast and effective, using sophisticated graphic design and special effects to help us see that this is a big-budget film that will be impressive and action-packed.

> **Website Extra!**
> There is an 'Editing techniques' information sheet, which explains each technique and its intended effect/impact, on the website.

> **Key Terms**
> **Prologue:** a pre-story sequence before the title credits begin
> **Fade-in:** the shot begins with a black screen and gradually fades into the image
> **Fade-out:** the shot ends with a gradual fading of the image to a black screen
> **Cut:** one shot ends and another begins
> **Pace:** the speed at which something happens or a story develops

Activity 7

Watch the opening 10 minutes of *Quantum of Solace*.

1. How does the prologue give the audience a sense of Bond's character and how he will react to situations later in the film?

2. Why is fast-paced editing used in action films?

3. What is the effect of cutting from close-up shots to long shots?

4. How does increasing the pace of the shot develop our understanding of potential danger and excitement of the scene?

Daniel Craig as James Bond in *Quantum of Solace* (2008).

ResultsPlus
Build better answers

Look at this part of a controlled assessment task:

In *Quantum of Solace* how are moving image techniques used to build a sense of tension?

■ A **Band 1** answer (1–2 marks) will **occasionally** use examples of moving image techniques such as describing the fade-in at the opening of the film but will show **limited understanding** of why it is used.

● A **Band 2** answer (3-5 marks) will select **some relevant examples**, such as the extreme close-up of Bond's eyes and show **some understanding** of how this is used to show that he is concentrating intensely on driving.

▲ A **Band 3** answer (6–7 marks) will select **relevant** and **convincing examples** that show **perceptive understanding**; for example, when explaining that it is important to capture the intensity of Bond's emotions the student would select the extreme close-up of his eyes and the sudden acceleration of pace to support this.

Choose a film from your controlled assessment focus genre.

① Watch the first ten minutes closely, pausing and rewinding the film so that you can focus on the small details.

② Write a paragraph analysing the editing techniques used in the opening of the film you have chosen. Use the case study on *Quantum of Solace* on page 29 as a guide.

Special effects

Special effects are used in a film to create a specific impact on the viewer. They are often eye-catching and memorable, but more importantly they help to draw the viewer's attention to a tense or emotional moment. Special effects can help the audience to understand more about character, theme and plot, as well as heighten an audience's emotional response to the film. Some special effects are small-scale, such as using special camera lenses or angles, but others are large-scale and very expensive.

Large-scale special effects require careful planning to create maximum impact. These include:

- **Set-pieces** – these are usually filmed with lots of cameras to get the best shots, e.g. the ship breaking in half in *Titanic* (1997). Here the audience will be impressed by the scale of the moment and be immersed in the drama and tragedy of it.

- **Explosions and fire** – these are always impressive special effects. An example is in *The Dark Knight* (2008) when the Joker walks out of a hospital which blows up behind him. The impact of the explosion makes the audience see how fearless and impressive the Joker is. We know that Batman has met his match and can expect a huge struggle.

- **CGI animation** – some effects are impossible (or too expensive) to create in real life. With developments in technology it has become possible to create characters, settings and effects on the computer screen and film them as if they existed in real life. *Avatar* (2009) was the first film using mostly CGI to be nominated for an Oscar.

Key Terms

Set-piece: usually a self-contained scene or sequence that stands on its own and serves as a key moment in the film

CGI (Computer Generated Imagery) animation: using computer graphics and technology in special effects

An example of some special effects used in *The Dark Knight*.

Activity 9

1 Watch the scene in *Transformers* (2007) where Sam Witwicky first sees his car turn into the transformer 'Bumblebee'.

   a) Note how the camera moves between Sam and the car – we realise something is happening before he does. How does this help to increase the tension that the audience feels?

   b) Notice how the camera switches between close-ups of the car and Sam's face. What is the impact on the audience of his realisation that something is happening?

   c) Finally, watch how the special effects of the transformation are created. What impact does this have on the audience?

2 Now watch a sequence that takes place at a key moment in a film from your controlled assessment focus genre. It could be a sad, happy, tense or exciting moment. Identify the techniques used to create visual impact.

ResultsPlus

Self assessment

Check your answer to question 2 in **Activity 9**. Have you:

- described specific uses of techniques used in the film?
- considered their effects on the audience?

Sound

Music, **dialogue** and **sound effects** combine to form the soundtrack of a moving image text.

Sometimes music is used to emphasise the atmosphere of a scene. For example, high-pitched string instruments might be used at a scary moment. Alternatively, calm, fluent music can enhance a happy atmosphere in the film.

Diegetic sound is any sound that is part of the film's world, such as when a character drops their keys and we hear them crash to the floor, or when someone speaks and we hear the words spoken. It is used mostly for realism – we know that sound is generated from a particular source, so if we see the source, we should hear the sound. For example, in *Toy Story* (1995) when Woody's voice cord is accidentally pulled and the noise alerts Sid's dog to chase them.

Non-diegetic sound is any sound that comes from outside the world of the film. This includes music used to create mood and atmosphere and sound effects that are added to create a dramatic effect. For example, when Simba's father dies in *The Lion King* (1994), powerful orchestral music emphasises the emotional impact of the scene.

Key Terms

Dialogue: words spoken by characters; it is scripted, rehearsed and delivered with close attention to the intended effects of the words on the viewer

Sound effect: noise that is used to create tension, to add drama or to emphasise realism, e.g. an explosion

Diegetic sound: sound that is created inside the story space/shot; usually used to emphasise realism, e.g. someone switches the radio on and we hear music

Non-diegetic sound: sound that is created outside the story space/shot; usually used to create mood or underline tension, e.g. orchestral music

Activity 10

Watch the sequence in *Titanic* where the ship is beginning to sink. We see the ship's designer, Andrews, drinking whisky by the fireplace and then an old couple lying side by side as water rushes in.

1 Focusing on the soundtrack, analyse the impact of this scene on the audience and explain how it has been achieved. Consider the following:

   a) How is diegetic sound used and what effect does it create on the audience?

   b) How is non-diegetic sound used and what effect does it create on the audience?

The dialogue or words spoken by characters are very important. The dialogue needs to be appropriate for the character, be relevant to the character and have a narrative purpose. This means the dialogue must move the story on and tell the audience something about the situation or characters.

When you look closely at the scene in a film you will also notice that the sound levels of words vary depending on whether a character is speaking close to the camera or far away. This can also create impact in the scene.

Activity 11

1. Watch the opening sequence of *Star Trek* (2009). Focus on the soundtrack and complete the table below to identify how music, dialogue and sound effects create impact. Some examples are given to help you.

Music	• Instantly recognisable theme tune from the TV series • •
Dialogue	• The captain speaks with powerful authority, showing he is a leader, while the words of others are heard only in the background • •
Sound effects	• The sound of the enemy spaceship appearing is dramatic and impressive • •

2. Now analyse the opening of a film from your controlled assessment focus genre. Write a paragraph analysing its soundtrack in the same way, commenting on music, dialogue and sound effects. Remember to show an awareness of the impact of diegetic and non-diegetic sound.

Film still from *Star Trek* (2009).

Opening sequences

Many films establish their style and identity during their opening sequences. The film-maker might use a logo or **ident** to reveal the genre to the audience. Other important elements in an opening sequence are the title, the establishing shot and the music.

- **Title** – important in establishing genre and style. Serious films with very realistic representations, such as emotional dramas, will often use serious titles such as *Panic Room* (2002). More light-hearted films may well suggest their genre through fun titles, such as *Legally Blonde* (2001).

- **Establishing shot** – shows the viewer where the film may be set and also gives clues about the film's genre. The film *Juno* (2007), for example, establishes immediately that the film is shot in small-town America with the clever use of animation to show our central character walking down the street and passing houses and shops. The focus on the teenage girl finding out she is pregnant suggests the film will be a drama.

- **Music** – another essential element in opening sequences as it immediately suggests genre and style.

> **Key Terms**
>
> **Ident:** like a logo, an instantly recognisable feature of a film, character or company

> **Website Extra!**
> Read the case study of the superhero film *The Dark Knight* (2007), to learn more about opening sequences.

Activity 12

Choose a film from your controlled assessment focus genre. Watch the opening sequence closely and identify the techniques used to give the film its own style and identity. What clues does it give to its audience about what it is about?

Preparing for your controlled assessment

In your controlled assessment task you will be asked a question about moving image techniques in the film you have studied. You will need to identify the techniques used by the film-maker to create meanings and messages that appeal to the audience and are appropriate for the theme, and for creating the mood and atmosphere. You will also need to explain how these techniques impact on the audience. To prepare for this question in relation to film language you should:

- Practise analysing film stills from your controlled assessment film genre so you become an expert in reading mise-en-scène.

- Choose key scenes from your chosen film and familiarise yourself with describing the setting, the characters, the props and the soundtrack.

- Practise identifying camera techniques – get used to using the correct terms and explaining why they might have been used in a particular moment.

- Familiarise yourself with editing and transition, and special effects techniques. Practise applying these techniques to scenes from your chosen film.

- Practise analysing soundtrack techniques relating to music, dialogue and sound effects during key moments of your chosen film.

4 Narrative structure

This chapter will help you to...

* understand how film narratives are structured to communicate meanings to their audiences

Key Terms

Narrative: a story or account

Narrative structure: the way a story is organised and shaped in terms of time and events

You will need to consider the narrative structure of your chosen film when responding to your controlled assessment task.

The word **narrative** means the way the story of a film is told, as well as the story itself. A **narrative structure** is the order in which the action takes place.

Many people have tried to analyse the best way to structure a narrative. One popular theory was put forward by Tzvetan Todorov. He outlined a basic structure that most narratives follow, as shown below.

1 A narrative usually begins with a stable world, known as the **Equilibrium**. At this stage we get a feel for the setting, meet the central character (the **protagonist**) and are given clues about the storyline.

2 Something happens to change the direction of the story. This is known as the **Disruption of the Equilibrium** or the **Inciting Incident**. The protagonist's world is disturbed. The story develops, becomes more complicated and we meet other characters.

3 The longest part of a narrative, known as the **Repairing of the Disruption**, involves sorting out the disruption and resolving the problem.

4 Events build up to a high point of tension and drama, known as the **Climax**.

5 After the Climax, the disruption is repaired and sorted out, and a new stable world, known as the **New Equilibrium**, is established.

The best way to see how this narrative structure works is to apply it to a film. This example below is from *Toy Story* (1995):

ResultsPlus
Watch out

Just telling the story of a film will get you very few marks. You need to explore the techniques used by the film-maker to help them tell the story. One of these techniques is the narrative structure.

> **Equilibrium**
> We are introduced to Woody and the other toys.

> **Disruption of the Equilibrium**
> Buzz Lightyear arrives and becomes Andy's new favourite toy instead of Woody.

> **Repairing of the Disruption**
> There is rivalry between Woody and Buzz, and they are separated from Andy.

> **Climax**
> Woody and Buzz work together to defeat Sid.

> **New Equilibrium**
> Woody and Buzz are reunited with Andy and the other toys.

In *Toy Story* the arrival of Buzz Lightyear is the Disruption of the Equilibrium.

In *Toy Story*, the presentation of the Disruption of the Equilibrium leads us to feel sympathy for Woody during the song 'Strange Things', which tells us the story of Buzz gradually replacing him as Andy's favourite toy. As Andy spends less time with Woody, changes his bedding to science-fiction patterns and chooses to cuddle Buzz when he goes to bed, we feel a real understanding of Woody's despair. This is emphasised by Woody's down-hearted expressions and slumped posture.

Activity 1

1 Match the events in the film *Juno* (2007) to the corresponding stages in the narrative structure.

| Equilibrium | Juno chooses the adoptive parents for her child and gets to know them. |

| Disruption of the Equilibrium | Juno goes into labour and gives birth to the baby. |

| Repairing of the Disruption | We are introduced to a young girl, Juno, who suspects she may be pregnant. She is on her way to the chemist. Her fast-talking narration shows us that she is intelligent and knows her own mind. |

| Climax | Juno confirms that she is pregnant and tells her boyfriend and parents that she intends to have the child adopted. |

| New Equilibrium | Even though the adoptive parents have split up, the adoptive mother takes the baby and Juno returns to her student life with her boyfriend. |

2 Choose a film from your controlled assessment focus genre and one of the narrative stages in the table above. What impact does this stage have on one of the characters?

Not all narratives fit into this straightforward structure. Some narratives contain unexpected surprises, making them more interesting and exciting for an audience. *The Time Traveler's Wife* (2009), for example, is about a man who jumps unpredictably through time and so the stages of the narrative are not in time order. Can you think of other examples of films with unusual narrative structures?

The term for something that does not fit the usual structure is a **subversion**. You may recognise some of these subversion techniques:

- **Flashback** – where a section of the film that happened in the past is referred back to, e.g. *The Incredible Hulk* (2008).

- **Flashforward** – where a section of the film from the future is shown before it would normally have happened, e.g. *Inside Man* (2006).

- **Twist** – where part of the film (often the end) is unpredictable or even shocking, e.g. *The Sixth Sense* (1999).

- **Parallel narratives** – where the lives of characters move alongside each other for some of the film without them meeting, e.g. *The Lake House* (2006).

Some film genres are more likely than others to have narrative subversion. For example, fantasy and science fiction are genres where the audience is likely to expect and accept the narrative more easily.

Key Terms

Subversion: when a technique is used which does not fit a theory or the usual way of doing something, e.g. when a twist takes the narrative in a new direction

ResultsPlus
Self assessment

Check your answer to **Activity 2**. Have you:

- explored the narrative techniques to show how the film-maker comments on a theme or creates a mood?
- considered how narrative techniques are used as part of genre?
- commented on how the narrative techniques are part of the genre's conventions, or challenge the genre conventions?

Activity 2

Choose a film from your controlled assessment film genre with narrative subversions.

1. What are the narrative subversions in your chosen film and how have they been used?

2. What messages do they communicate to the target audience?

3. Why do you think its narrative has been subverted?

Preparing for your controlled assessment

In your controlled assessment task you will need to consider narrative structure when responding to questions about the characters, moving image techniques and genre. To prepare for these questions in relation to the narrative you should:

- Learn the stages of a narrative and make sure you can apply them to your chosen film and one other film from the same genre.

- Choose the key moments from both your chosen film and the comparative film that show the narrative stages.

- Make sure you can discuss the main themes in your chosen film – how are the themes treated? What messages is the film-maker communicating to the audience?

- Explore any narrative subversions that your chosen film and one other film from the same genre use for impact and effect.

- What are some typical narratives in your controlled assessment film genre? Make sure you can comment on how typical or challenging the narrative is in your chosen film and one other film from the same genre.

5 Representation

In your controlled assessment task you will analyse the ways in which people, places, events and issues or themes are shown (or represented) in moving image texts. You will also be asked questions about characters in the film you have studied. Analysing **representations** will help you to decide how and why texts have been created, and what messages they are communicating to audiences.

Representations of people are usually designed to make them as believable as possible, but if you look closely at representations of key social groups such as women, men, teenagers, ethnic communities or older people, you will see that they are often **stereotypes**. Many representations of teenagers, for example, show them as being disrespectful, moody and selfish – this is obviously a very narrow view of teenagers!

The film-maker's choices can have a major impact on the audience. For example, traditional Disney films often use stereotypes in the same way that fairy tales do: they reproduce certain roles in society and teach children how they are meant to act in certain situations.

When a representation is deliberately created to try to influence the audience, it is known as a **biased representation**. Superhero films tend to use this. For example, in the *Superman* series (1978–2006), Clark Kent is represented as good and Lex Luther is represented as evil.

> **This chapter will help you to...**
>
> * understand what representation means
> * make connections between representations and bias
> * see how representation affects character types and their role in a film

> **Key Terms**
>
> **Representation:** how people, places, events or ideas are shown to audiences in media texts
>
> **Stereotypes:** showing groups of people in terms of certain widely held but oversimplified characteristics: for example, showing women as nagging housewives
>
> **Biased representation:** a representation that is deliberately created to influence an audience

Activity 1

1. Select three of these social groups: men, women, children under 10, teenage boys, teenage girls, families, the elderly.

2. Find examples of the different ways in which films from a range of genres represent your chosen social groups. You could look at some of the following films as a starting point:

   * *Up* (2009)
   * *Twilight* (2008)
   * *Ocean's Eleven* (2001)
   * *Avatar* (2009)
   * *The Truman Show* (1998)
   * *Valentine's Day* (2010)

3. Share your research with others in your class. Decide which representations are the most and least stereotypical.

Audiences often find meanings in films by engaging with the central characters, learning and accepting their viewpoints and identifying with their reactions to different situations. Analysing the representations of characters in the films you are studying should play an important part in your preparation for your controlled assessment.

Look at the images below of two film characters. These images show typical representations of teenage boys in high school. The first image shows a sporty, popular teenager. His jacket shows that he is in a sports team, and his clothing and hair look fashionable. The second image is of a high-school 'geek', with curly hair, glasses and high-waisted trousers.

Zack Siler from *She's All That* (1999) is a 'high-school jock'.

Controlled assessment tip

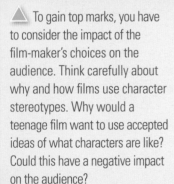

△ To gain top marks, you have to consider the impact of the film-maker's choices on the audience. Think carefully about why and how films use character stereotypes. Why would a teenage film want to use accepted ideas of what characters are like? Could this have a negative impact on the audience?

Napoleon Dynamite is an unpopular high-school student who wants to fit in (*Napoleon Dynamite*, 2004).

Activity 2

1. Choose one of the following films that you know well or choose a favourite film of your own:

   - *X Men 3: The Last Stand* (2006)
   - *Juno* (2007)
   - Any James Bond film
   - Any Disney film

2. Describe how two of the central characters in the film are represented. You may wish to comment on:

   - their clothing
   - their relationships with others
   - their speech and behaviour
   - their role in the film and how that affects their representation.

3. Now explain which of your chosen representations are the most and least stereotypical.

4. Finally, try to explain how the ways in which the characters are represented have an effect on how audiences see them.

Character types

It has been suggested that there are only a limited number of character types in any film genre, each of which has their own purpose in a moving image narrative. These character types include:

- **Hero** – the central character (or **protagonist**) of the narrative whose story we follow and who has some kind of challenge to undertake in return for a reward. The hero is traditionally male, e.g. Superman, but in modern narratives can be female, e.g. Lara Croft.

- **Heroine** – acts as a reward for the hero for succeeding with the challenge; often the hero and heroine have a romantic attachment! In modern narratives, the heroine is often quite feisty and helps the hero with the challenge, e.g. Uhuru in *Star Trek* (2009).

- **Villain** (or **antagonist**) – seeks riches, glory and/or power, and also seeks to stop the hero from succeeding with his or her challenge. They can be male, e.g. Magneto in the *X-Men* films, or female, e.g. Ursula in *The Little Mermaid* (1989).

- **Donor** or **mentor** – gives the hero important information or equipment to help him or her in the challenge. They are often wise or have special powers, e.g. Optimus Prime in the *Transformers* films or Obi Wan Kenobi in the *Star Wars* films.

> **Key Terms**
>
> **Protagonist:** the central character in a film
>
> **Antagonist:** the main villain in a film who is in conflict with the protagonist

Optimus Prime is the mentor to hero Sam Witwicky in *Transformers*.

Website Extra!
A worksheet is available to fill in for Activity 3.

Activity 3

1. Choose **one** of the character types listed on page 39 (e.g. hero or villain). Find examples of that type of character in films from the following genres, then make notes on what we learn about these characters in the films you have chosen.

   - Romantic comedy
   - Historical drama
   - Action
   - Crime
   - Comedy

You will have noticed in Activity 3 that characters of each type may be male in some genres and female in others. You will also have noticed other subtle differences, such as the fact that the hero character is not always brave or good-looking – or even human!

This close observation is what you will need to use to explore the representations of character types in your controlled assessment. Keep in mind two questions:

1. What impact does this representation have on the viewer?

2. What messages are being communicated to the audience through this character?

It is often through our identification with characters that the film-maker can communicate messages to audiences. In the *X-Men* films, for example, the character of Professor Xavier is a donor/mentor type who is shown as being wise, kind and compassionate. He is also in a wheelchair. This gives a message to the audience that such qualities are valuable and do not depend on health, strength or prosperity.

ResultsPlus
Watch out

■ Don't refer to the characters in films as if they are real people. You need to think about them as choices made by a film-maker to communicate ideas and themes.

Website Extra!
You can read more about character types on the website.

Activity 4

Look again at your chosen character type from Activity 3.

1. Make notes on the messages that are communicated from the characters' representations in different genres.

Intertextuality

When watching a film, have you ever recognised an **allusion** to another film or story? This type of link between two texts is known as an **intertextual reference**. Films such as *Date Movie* (2006), *Toy Story* (1995) and *Shrek* (2001) all allude to other films. The film *The League of Extraordinary Gentlemen* (2003) uses intertextual references to many literary novels. Can you name any of the intertextual references used in these films?

Do you recognise the phrase 'Beam me up Scotty'? This is associated with the *Star Trek* films and television programmes. The phrase has also been used in advertisements, comic strips and even in major films such as *Armageddon* (1998).

Another example of an intertextual phrase is 'I am your father'. This was originally used in the *Star Wars* films and has more recently been included in *Toy Story 2* (1999) and the *Austin Powers* films.

> ### Key Terms
> **Allusion:** a reference or link to another text without actually naming that text
> **Intertextual reference:** when one media text mimics or refers to another media text in a way that many consumers will recognise

Activity 5

1. Why do you think intertextual phrases like the examples given above are used? What effect will they have on the audience?

Intertextual references can also be visual. In *Toy Story 2*, the toys are riding around Al's Toy Barn in a Barbie tour guide car. Rex the dinosaur is running behind them, his reflection clearly seen in the wing mirror. This is an intertextual reference to the scene in *Jurassic Park* (1993) when the T-Rex can be seen in the wing mirror chasing the tour guide vehicle.

Bridget Jones's Diary (2001) is full of intertextual references to Jane Austen's *Pride and Prejudice*. Although the settings and the characters are very different, the basic storyline is similar: girl meets and hates boy but after many mishaps falls in love with him and marries him.

Audiences enjoy intertextuality because when they recognise an allusion to another text they feel involved in the film and able to appreciate what they are watching on more than one level. Intertextuality may be used for humour, or as a way for a film-maker to pay tribute to another film-maker.

The film series *Shrek* uses many intertextual references.

Iconography

Iconography is an important part of representation in films. Iconography can be used to help the audience identify genre. Some objects, images, characters and settings are iconic for different genres. For example:

- a ticking clock to emphasise the race against time in an action film
- the destruction of an important landmark building in a disaster film
- spaceships in a science-fiction film
- cowboys in a western.

The film-maker will sometimes use iconography as a short cut in a plot but it can also be used to suggest a more complex idea.

When trying to give a sense of setting to the audience the film-maker might choose a recognisable location to act as an icon for that setting. The location can be used in an establishing shot, letting the audience know where the action is taking place. However, the setting might also be used to suggest meanings to the audience. Using a recognisable location that already has meanings for the audience adds to the messages in the film.

The ending of the film *Sleepless in Seattle* (1993) takes place at the top of the Empire State building. This suggests romance and a happy ending because the Empire State building has a romantic image. The building has views over the city of New York, which is an aspirational city of America – the city represents dreams and the feeling that anything is possible.

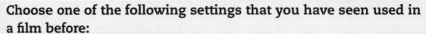

Activity 6

Choose one of the following settings that you have seen used in a film before:

- **Central Park in New York**
- **The Eiffel Tower in Paris**
- **The Big Ben clock tower in London.**

1. List three films that have used your chosen setting.

2. Explain how each of the films that you have listed uses this setting. Is it an establishing shot or does the film use the setting to add greater meaning to the story?

Central Park in New York

The Eiffel Tower in Paris.

Big Ben in London.

Iconography is not limited to the setting. Objects or suggestions of objects can also be used to convey a complex idea. For example, trees can be used to suggest ideas about knowledge and life but also attitudes to the environment.

Activity 7

Look at the film stills below from *The Lord of the Rings: The Fellowship of the Ring* (2001) and *300* (2007).

Still from *The Lord of the Rings: The Fellowship of the Ring*.

Still from *300*.

1. Research the films to explore why the film-maker chose to use the icon of the tree.

2. Look at the two stills again. The use of colour and the use of light in the shots could also be considered iconic. Discuss with a partner other choices made by the film-makers that could have a deeper meaning.

Preparing for your controlled assessment

In your controlled assessment task you will be asked a question about the characters in your chosen film. To prepare for this question you should:

- Make connections between the characters featured in your chosen film and the social groups that they represent in real life.

- Practise writing about the characters as stereotypical or challenging representations of those social groups.

- Explore how audiences identify with characters in films – from their appearance, to their behaviour, to their role in the film and the likely effects of their 'journey' on the audience.

- Learn the main character types and their function in a film narrative – apply these to the characters in your chosen film.

- Make connections between the characters in your chosen film and the messages that a film-maker might be communicating to the audience through the ways the characters are represented.

Controlled Assessment Practice

How will I be assessed?

You will be assessed under controlled conditions for this unit, which is worth 20% of your final mark. This means that you can prepare in class with your teacher and classmates, but you will have to write your response to the task individually in controlled conditions. You may take notes into your controlled assessment but these will be checked by your teacher.

Edexcel will set the tasks that you will complete. There will be a choice of two genres each year (for example, science-fiction and comedy), with a choice of two tasks for each genre, each on a different film. It is likely that your teacher will choose which genre and film you will study as a class.

You will have up to **three** hours in controlled conditions to complete the tasks.
You will be expected to produce a written response of up to **1000 words**.

What am I being assessed on?

There are two Assessment Objectives for this unit:

AO1 Read and understand digital communication in a range of contexts, selecting relevant textual detail appropriate to purpose – this is asking you to select examples from the films and talk about the meaning of the specific examples that you have chosen.

AO2 Analyse and evaluate how digital communication is designed to achieve effects and to engage and influence the audience – this asks you to consider how the moving image techniques are used to have an impact on the audience. You will need to think about:

- how the audience are expected to react
- what techniques are being used to engage their attention.

How can I succeed in this assessment?

To succeed in the assessment you need to:

✓ have a thorough knowledge of the film named in the task

✓ be familiar with at least one other film in the same genre

✓ think carefully about the sequence given in Section A and select an appropriate second sequence in Section B

✓ focus on moving image techniques used in both sequences and consider their impact on the audience

✓ do some research to make sure you have a thorough understanding of your chosen genre and the conventions associated with it.

Sample controlled assessment task

GENRE 1: Science Fiction ....

> There will be a choice of two genres. You or your teacher should select one of the genres and one of the two tasks on films within that genre.

Task 1 *Star Wars: The Phantom Menace Episode 1*
Cert PG (20th Century Fox, 1999)

Section A: Close textual analysis

Responses to Section A should be based on a detailed study of the following sequence from the DVD.

> You will be able to watch this extract as many times as you like during your preparation for this task.

In point: Shot of a spacecraft approaching a planet.
Out point: After the aliens close the blast doors and say 'That will hold them!'

In this sequence from the film, what does the audience learn about the two Ambassadors? ....

> Whatever genre you are studying, this question will always ask you to comment on what the audience learns about something, such as a character or characters.

(Total for Section A = 10 marks)

Section B: Analysing moving image

Choose a short sequence of about 2–3 minutes from *Star Wars: The Phantom Menace* which has a sense of excitement.

In this sequence, how are moving image techniques used by the director to create a sense of excitement?

In your response, you must:

- identify moving image techniques used by the director
- select appropriate examples of where these techniques are used ....
- comment on the effects of these techniques on the audience.

> These bullet points help you meet the Assessment Objectives. They also make a good structure for a paragraph, following the pattern of PEE or PQD, which you may have been taught in English.

(Total for Section B = 14 marks)

Section C: Understanding genre

(i) In what ways does *Star Wars: The Phantom Menace* conform to, or challenge, the conventions of the Science Fiction genre?

(8)

> Here you need to write about a second film. Think carefully about choosing a film that plays with the rules of the genre you have selected. A film that does something slightly different with the rules might be more interesting to write about!

(ii) Choose **one other** moving image text from the Science Fiction genre. ....

Explore how the director of your chosen moving image text uses the conventions of the Science Fiction genre.

(8)

(Total for Section C = 16 marks) ....

> Look carefully at the marks for each section. Try to spend more time and effort on the 16 mark question than on the 10 mark question.

Maximise your marks

Here are some extracts from student answers to a controlled assessment task on the comedy genre, focusing on the film *Toy Story* (1995). Read the answers and the examiner comments. They will help you to improve your marks.

Section A: Close textual analysis

Responses to Section A should be based on a detailed study of the following sequence from the DVD.

In point: Buzz Lightyear 'Where's that bonding strip'
Out point: Woody falls to the floor laughing.

In this sequence from the film, what does the audience learn about the characters of Buzz Lightyear and Woody?

(10 marks)

Student 1 – Extract typical of a grade Ⓒ answer

This is a good use of words from the question that shows understanding about the text. However, it would have been better to start with what the film-maker was attempting to do with this character rather than describing something from the scene.

> You learn that Buzz Lightyear thinks he is really a spaceman. You know this because he thinks he is going to choke when Woody opens his helmet and Woody makes fun of him for thinking he is real. The audience are meant to find this funny because Buzz Lightyear doesn't really get what Woody is talking about and we think he is stupid.

This mention of the audience shows the student has thought about impact. The comments just need to go into a little more depth.

Examiner summary

This part of the answer is typical of grade C performance. The choice of the example, when the helmet is opened, does support the point being made about the character Buzz Lightyear. However, other examples would have allowed for a stronger comment; for example, Buzz's serious response to Woody. The student's comments show understanding of impact but they need to go into more detail to improve the answer.

Student 2 – Extract typical of a grade Ⓐ answer

This is an insightful point that is well explained using examples from the text.

> The director of the film is using Buzz Lightyear as a foil for Woody's humour in this sequence. Buzz is portrayed as deluded as he believes he is the real Buzz Lightyear. He has bought so much into his role that he even thinks he might choke if his helmet is removed. The seriousness with which he speaks to Woody and his straight-faced concern over the alien acts as a perfect contrast to Woody, making the sequence funnier.

The extra detail here shows a very good understanding of Buzz's role in this scene.

Examiner summary

This part of the answer is typical of grade A performance. The student makes an insightful point about Buzz's role in this scene, noting that Buzz's seriousness and delusion is a means of creating humour in this scene. This point is well developed and the example of the alien is particularly well chosen.

Section B: Analysing moving image

Choose a short sequence of about 2—3 minutes from *Toy Story* in which humour is created.

In this sequence, how are moving image techniques used by the director to create humour?

In your response, you must:

- identify moving image techniques used by the director
- select appropriate examples of where these techniques are used
- comment on the effects of these techniques on the audience.

(14 marks)

Student 1 – Extract typical of a grade (C) answer

> This is a good identification of moving image techniques, with appropriate examples selected.

Later in the film Woody and Buzz are captured by the neighbourhood boy. They are trapped in his house. The director uses a close-up of the boy through the magnifying glass in order to exaggerate his evilness. The dramatic music in the background is also like one of those films where there is a villain and so makes the audience link to the old fashioned films with heroes and villains. It seems to be making fun of these films.

> This is the beginning of a good comment on impact, but it hasn't been developed clearly enough to gain higher marks.

Examiner summary

This part of the answer is typical of grade C performance. The examples selected (the use of the close-up and the music) are appropriate and help to back up the point being made. The comments on the impact are good, but the student believes they have made the connection between the examples selected and the idea of calling on a different type of film. To improve this answer the student needs to make this link more obvious.

Student 2 – Extract typical of a grade (A) answer

> This is a very good point and the comment about the exaggerated music makes it relevant to the question.

The director cleverly uses allusion to other films to bring comedy to the film. When the neighbourhood boy is torturing Woody there is music similar to that found on Star Wars and the boy's dialogue refers to 'rebels'. This is exaggerated in Toy Story, parodying the good guy/bad guy dynamic of the Star Wars films. There is also reference to The Wizard of Oz when Woody hysterically repeats 'there is no place like home' on the way down the stairs. This allusion adds humour to the film because the audience laugh at the way the director has parodied the original film by exaggerating it in this situation. It also adds interest to the film as the audience are constantly linking to the original film.

> The use of more than one example helps to show that the student has in-depth understanding.

Examiner summary

This part of the answer is typical of grade A performance. The student has made a very insightful point about allusions to other films. The level of detail that the student has included is important in achieving a higher mark. Specific reference to lines from the film demonstrates a very effective use of relevant examples.

Section C: Understanding genre

(i) In what ways does *Toy Story* conform to, or challenge, the conventions of the Comedy genre?

(8 marks)

Student 1 – Extract typical of a grade C answer

There is a good use of technical terms but it might have been better to focus on one of these and use examples for each.

Toy Story uses many conventions of comedy. It uses many different types of comedy such as slapstick, foils and play on words. The film also ends happily which is characteristic of a comedy. At the end Buzz and Woody are friends when throughout the film they have been rivals but even then the film is funny because Andy gets a puppy and the audience are asked to imagine the sort of trouble the boys will get into next.

There is good focus on the audience and the impact the choices have.

Examiner summary

This part of the answer is typical of grade C performance. The student uses some clever technical terms and this is important. However, the answer is a little general and there is a need for more specific examples.

Student 2 – Extract typical of a grade A answer

This is an excellent opening that focuses on the overall effect of comedy.

Toy Story is a conventional comedy, mostly because its aim is to make the viewer laugh. The most common form of comedy used is a play on the idea of toys. For example, Mr Potato Head's features keep changing and the incident where the toy soldier falls down and can't get back up because his feet are glued together. Also characteristic of a comedy is a happy ending. At the end of Toy Story Buzz and Woody become friends, resolving the conflict that has been the main focus of the humour throughout the film.

There is a clever use of specific examples from different points of the film that shows a detailed understanding.

Examiner summary

This part of the answer is typical of grade A performance. This is a clever response balancing an overall idea of comedy with relevant specific examples from different points in the film. The comments on the impact of these choices are explored in some detail.

(ii) Choose one other moving image text from the Comedy genre.

Explore how the director of your chosen moving image text uses the conventions of the Comedy genre.

(8 marks)

Student 1 – Extract typical of a grade Ⓒ answer

> Lots of relevant examples have been selected but these have not really been explored so the response feels descriptive.

The film *Up* uses the conventions of a comedy such as the young scout who goes along with the old man and ends up on the outside of the house when it took off. Also, the dogs who can speak are funny. It is particularly amusing when the Doberman speaks in a high voice. This is funny because it is the opposite of what we expect. This means it is conventional because it uses unusual or unexpected events to make the audience laugh. *Up* is unusual for a comedy because it is quite sad, especially the first ten minutes when his wife died and when he lets the house go.

> This is a good point but it needs to be explained further to achieve a higher mark.

Examiner summary

This part of the answer is typical of grade C performance. This response has the potential to be an excellent answer. The relevant parts of the film have been selected and there is some comment on how the film impacts on the audience. However, to get a higher mark the student needs to link the ideas together more.

Student 2 – Extract typical of a grade Ⓐ answer

Up uses unusual and extraordinary situations to create comic effect. The idea that a man can blow up enough balloons that his house can float is peculiar and this is what leads to much of the comedy. The comedy moments are emphasised by a music soundtrack that becomes light-hearted and bouncy when something funny is happening. Also, the director includes ironic characters such as the squeaky voiced Doberman to play with the expectations of the audience. Like many comedies *Up* is filled with pathos, where the humour is used to highlight the sadness of the grieving husband and the release of the house at the end is supposed to be uplifting, fulfilling the conventional idea of a happy ending.

> This is a good, specific reference to moving image techniques used by the film-maker.

> The use of sophisticated vocabulary helps to persuade the examiner that the response is insightful.

Examiner summary

This part of the answer is typical of grade A performance. The student has commented on techniques used by the film-maker and has used technical vocabulary to impress on the marker that this is a sophisticated response.

Unit 2 Developing skills in critical reading

To be literate in the 21st century means being skilled and confident in reading, assessing and creating different forms of digital texts, as well as being confident with traditional printed texts.

In this student book unit you will study the following types of digital text:

- websites
- blogs
- digital video
- social networking
- podcasts
- mobile communication.

You will need to:

- identify the intended audience and purpose of the text
- consider the choices made by the writer
- analyse the strengths and weaknesses of the text.

Your assessment

Unit 2 is an examination unit. The examination will last **1 hour 45 minutes** and is divided into two sections:

Section A: Unseen texts – this part of the examination includes questions on two digital texts that you have not previously studied. You will be asked to analyse the texts and will be asked questions about the intended audience and purpose, the features and the effectiveness of the texts. You will also be asked to choose what digital text you would advise someone to use to fulfil a brief and explain the reasons for your choice.

Section B: Pre-released texts – your teacher will be sent details of six different digital texts before your examination and you will study these together. One of these texts will appear on the examination paper. You will be asked questions about the components, how the text achieves its aims, and the strengths and weaknesses of the text. You will also be asked to choose what digital texts could be used effectively to fulfil a brief and explain the reasons for your choice.

Assessment Objectives

Your examination will be marked using these Assessment Objectives:

AO1 Read and understand digital communication in a range of contexts, selecting relevant textual detail appropriate to purpose.

AO2 Analyse and evaluate how digital communication is designed to achieve effects and to engage and influence the audience/reader.

1 Audience and purpose

In your examination you will be asked questions about the intended **audience** and **purpose** of a digital text you have not previously studied.

Identifying the intended audience of a text means working out who the digital text is aimed at – who the reader, listener or viewer is likely to be. You should consider two key questions when thinking about the intended audience:

1 Who does the digital text seem to be aimed at? The audience group might be defined by age, gender or interests, for example.

2 What does the digital text assume about its readers – what are their interests, knowledge and attitudes?

Identifying the purpose of a digital text means working out why it has been created. There are many words you can use to describe a text's purpose. These could include:

* to inform – for example, a news report
* to entertain – for example, a video on YouTube
* to communicate – for example, an update on a social network site.

Remember that a digital text can have more than one purpose.

Look at the home page of *Sugar* magazine's website below.

Activity 1

Study the home page of *Sugar*'s online magazine on page 52.

① Identify the intended audience(s) of the online magazine.

② Identify the purpose(s) of the online magazine.

③ What clues did you use to identify the audience(s) and purpose(s)?

> **Key Term**
> **Features:** anything that relates to the presentation, layout or language of a digital text

You will also need to comment on the **features** of a digital text and explain the impact of these features on the audience in your examination.

The audience and purpose influence the choices the writer makes when producing their text. These choices include:

- selecting still or moving images
- deciding on the design and presentation
- making language choices.

Digital texts are carefully created to appeal to their target audience. Many producers of digital texts research their audiences to find out what is important to them. They then make sure that the design and presentation of their texts appeal to the audience and have the impact they intended.

When writing about the impact of a digital text you should explain how the features contribute to the text's meanings and messages, fulfil the text's purpose and appeal to the intended audience.

ResultsPlus
Exam tip

⚠ When you look at the texts in your examination, always ask yourself how they relate to the needs and lifestyle of their audiences.

Activity 2

Look again at the home page of *Sugar*'s online magazine.

① What messages does it give to its intended audience?

> *It assumes that the audience might be anxious about their appearance as there are fashion and beauty tips...*

② Identify three features that communicate these messages.

> *The site uses friendly, casual language like 'cool trousers' because...*

Key Term

Aspiration: hope or ambition to achieve an image or lifestyle, e.g. to be popular, to have a fast car, to be seen as kind and generous

When an audience sees something that they wish they could have or become, we say that they 'aspire' to it. For example, by reading about fashion, accessories and celebrity lifestyles in an online magazine, an audience may aspire to that kind of life. The text on the *Sugar* website builds on the audience's **aspirations**.

Website Extra!

Links to the websites given in Activity 3 are available on the website.

Website Extra!

'Grabbing' a screen is an easy way to capture interesting digital texts to help you prepare for the examination. To learn how to do this on a PC and a Mac, download the information sheet.

Activity 3

Choose one of the following digital texts:

- **CBBC home page**
- **Stardoll home page**
- **Disney home page**

1 Take a screen grab of your chosen text and paste it into a document. Answer the following questions about the website:

a) Who is the most likely audience of the site? Does it target both girls and boys? Does it seem most suited to a certain age range?

b) What is the purpose of the site? Is it to entertain, to inform, to persuade, to promote something, or to raise awareness of a situation?

c) What needs and lifestyle is the audience likely to have? For example, does the audience need to have information on interactive games, fashion or image, new films?

2 Make notes on how the writer of the site has appealed to its audience.

Results Plus
Build better answers

Look at this examination question:

Explain how the writer has appealed to the audience of Text A.

■ A **Band 1** answer (1-2 marks) will show only **basic understanding** of the audience, picking out little from the text and making **little comment** on the meaning intended by the writer. It is likely that there will be very little written in response to the question.

● A **Band 2** answer (3 marks) will have a **sound understanding** of the audience, showing they can **make reference** to features to support **relevant comments**. This answer will obviously answer the question.

▲ A **Band 3** answer (4 marks) will have a **developed understanding** of the audience of the text. Features selected will be **effective** in allowing the student to provide **detailed comment** on the intended meaning of the writer. The answer will explore more than the obvious points, showing that the student has thought things through.

Remember that in the examination you will be asked to select and explain the features used in a digital text that help to convey the main messages and meanings for the intended audience.

Activity 4

Study the screen grab from The Box home page.

Answer the questions below.

1. What features are used on this page?

    > The use of the graffiti font on the wall...

2. Who is the intended audience and what is the purpose of this page? How did you work this out?

3. What messages about The Box does this page give to its audience?

4. How do the features help to achieve this message?

In the examination you will be asked to explain how you can effectively use digital texts to fulfil a brief.

One technique that producers of digital texts use to attract a greater audience is to use links and advertisements. These encourage the audience to browse further texts. For example, Googlemail scans key words that are written in e-mails and provides **bespoke** advertisements related to these key words. Facebook does the same. Shopping websites record what you have bought and provide suggestions of other products you might like.

Key Term

Bespoke: written or adapted for a specific user or purpose

Activity 5

As a class, carry out the following survey.

1. How does this use of advertising impact on the way you might use digital texts if you were:

   • trying to keep young people safe online
   • trying to promote a new band to a wide audience
   • trying to buy something online.

Key Term

Intertextual links: when one media text links or refers to another media text

Digital texts often create **intertextual links** with other texts through references, hyperlinks, intertextual advertising, etc. For example, audiences may begin looking at a newspaper site and then move on to watching a moving image, checking sports results and reading news stories of their local area on different sites in very different texts.

Activity 6

Browse the *EastEnders* website.

1. How many different digital texts can you access through the website?

2. Why do you think the creators of the site make it possible for you to use the site in so many different ways?

3. What responses do you think audiences might have towards *EastEnders* as a result of using this site?

Audience-generated content

Audiences of digital texts do not just read, watch or listen to the text – they are also able to contribute to the content of the digital text. Some digital texts are even created entirely by the audience!

A **wiki** is an example of a digital text that is created by the audience. Users can create new content, edit it and make changes to other users' contributions. Wikis enable people to share information and can be easily updated. The biggest example of a wiki is the online encyclopedia Wikipedia.

> **Key Term**
>
> **Wiki:** a website that allows users to add and update their own content on the site. Wiki is a Hawaiian word meaning 'fast' and is often used to stand for 'What I need to Know Is'

Activity 7

Study a wiki site, such as Wikipedia.

1 What is the purpose of wiki sites like Wikipedia?

2 What are the strengths and weaknesses of such sites?

Wikis are also used in schools. Study this image of a school wiki site.

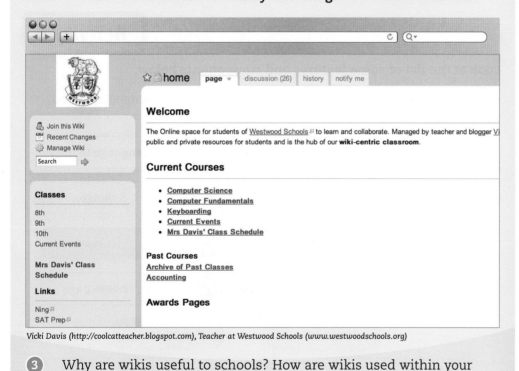

Vicki Davis (http://coolcatteacher.blogspot.com), Teacher at Westwood Schools (www.westwoodschools.org)

3 Why are wikis useful to schools? How are wikis used within your school or college?

Preparing for your examination

When preparing for your examination:

- Remember that being able to identify the intended audience(s) and purpose(s) of a digital text is an essential part of responding to the two unseen texts you will be given in Section A.

- Remember to link the features of the unseen texts to the impact on the audience.

- Practise commenting on how effective different digital texts are in achieving their purpose.

2 Features, components and messages

Key Terms

Features: anything that relates to the presentation, layout or language of a digital text

Components: those elements that make the text work, e.g. links, home pages, icons, moving images

Features and components

You will be asked in the examination to identify three features and three components of a digital text. You will also need to explain the impact and use of these features and components.

You have already learned that digital texts combine features and components.

* **Features** are anything that relate to presentation, layout or language.
* **Components** are those elements that make the text work. They might relate to the functionality of the text, such as how the user navigates through the text using the home page, links and buttons, or make up the text itself, such as the soundtrack or a video.

It is important to distinguish between the features and components of digital texts. In Section A of your examination (Unseen texts) you will focus on features; in Section B (Pre-released texts) you will focus on components.

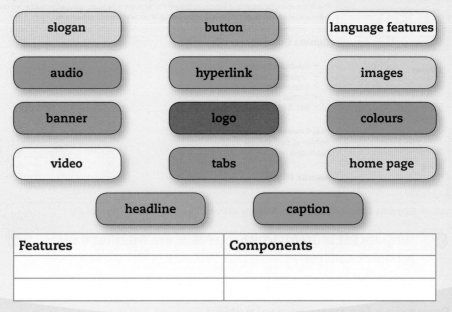

Activity 1

Look at the list of some features and components below.

1. Decide which are features and which are components and record your answers in a copy of the table.

slogan	button	language features
audio	hyperlink	images
banner	logo	colours
video	tabs	home page
	headline	caption

Features	Components

2. Add three more examples of features and components to your table.

Website Extra!
A table with the correct answers for Activity 1 is available to download. Use it when you revise digital text components.

Sometimes the distinction between features and components is not straight forward. An image can be both a feature and a component. When commenting on an image as a feature, you need to focus on the details of that image, such as the colours used, the expressions of the subject and the composition. When discussing the image as a component, you need to consider how the image is used within the text and how it combines with other components to make the text work.

Digital texts can also become components of another digital text. For example, podcasts and digital videos could be included as components of a website.

Messages

The **message** of a digital text is the intended impact, meaning or effect of the features and components. The producer of a digital text will choose carefully which features and components to use to:

- appeal to the intended audience
- achieve the purpose of the text
- communicate the message of the text.

A digital text producer might use images to communicate the message of the text. Images are often used to influence audiences because they can communicate very powerful messages.

Activity 2

Study this award-winning photograph taken by US photographer Dorothea Lange in 1936. It is called 'Migrant Mother'.

1. What is the overall effect of the photograph on you?

2. Study the features of this image and answer the following questions:

   a) Why do you think the photograph is in black and white?

   b) Look at how the image has been composed: the woman is shown with her three children. How are they shown to us and what do we understand by this?

   c) Focus on the mother herself. She holds her face and looks into the distance with a serious expression on her face. How does this affect you, the audience?

3. Now consider this image as a component of a digital text.

   - How could this image be used within a digital text? What impact would this image have on the audience?

   - How could the image be used with other components to communicate the message of the digital text?

Preparing for your examination

When preparing for your examination:

- Make sure you can discuss the features (presentation elements) and components (working elements) of each type of digital text.
- Practise explaining how the use of features and components communicate messages to the audience(s).

3 Conventions

Key Terms

Conventions: operating rules which apply in particular text types and aid audience recognition and understanding

In your examination you will be asked to choose appropriate digital texts to fulfil a brief. To do this you will need to understand the **conventions** or operating rules of different types of digital text.

Activity 1

Working in small groups, choose one of the scenarios from the list below:

* **dining at an expensive restaurant**
* **swimming at a public pool**
* **giving a short talk to your whole class.**

1. Make a list of three DOs and three DON'Ts to advise someone who is going to experience your chosen scenario for the first time.

You probably found that you had an immediate sense of the rules – or conventions – that apply in the scenarios in Activity 1.

It is important that you understand the difference between features, components, messages and conventions.

* **Features** are anything to do with the text's presentation, layout or language (see Chapters 1 and 2).
* **Components** are anything that relate to the functionality of the digital text, such as links, home pages or moving images (see Chapter 2).
* **Messages** are the intended impact, meaning or effect on the audience of the features and components (see Chapters 1 and 2).
* **Conventions** help to shape the digital text's meanings by calling on the audience's own knowledge of how texts work.

The conventions of a text will also depend on the type of text being produced. There are different categories for types of text, including:

* business/commercial purposes (e.g. selling items, travel, advertising)
* charity
* personal uses (user-generated content)
* public information (e.g. council website)
* politics (news and current affairs)
* education
* leisure and entertainment.

The digital text you study in preparation for your examination will be taken from one of these categories.

Results Plus
Examiner tip

⚠ It is important to remember the difference between **features**, **components**, **messages** and **conventions**. Do not get these mixed up in the examination!

You already know that you will be studying six types of digital text for your examination. Each of these texts has its own conventions. These help producers and writers to make digital texts that audiences will recognise and understand.

Activity 2

Look at the features and components below, which can be used to make up the conventions of different digital texts.

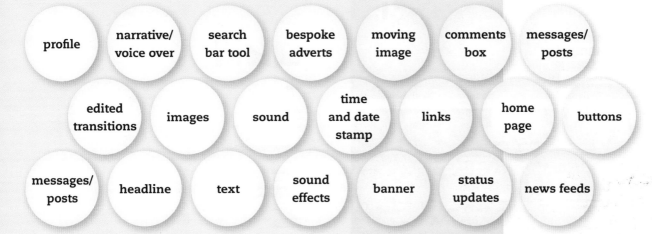

profile • narrative/voice over • search bar tool • bespoke adverts • moving image • comments box • messages/posts • edited transitions • images • sound • time and date stamp • links • home page • buttons • messages/posts • headline • text • sound effects • banner • status updates • news feeds

1 Using the features and components listed above, copy and complete the table below to list the conventions of each digital text type.

Website	Digital video	Podcast	Blog	Social networking	Mobile communication
images sound moving image links buttons...					

2 Add as many other conventions to your table as you can.

Activity 3

Divide into six groups. Each group should choose one of the digital texts on page 62 and make a list of the conventions that apply to that type of digital text. Use the links on the website to explore your chosen digital text in more detail.

1 To help you do this, answer the following questions:

a) What do you expect to find in your chosen digital text type?

b) What do you recognise as being typical of your chosen digital text?

c) Is there anything different or unusual about your chosen digital text?

2 Feed back your findings (you can discuss them or make notes). Make sure that you understand the conventions of each type of digital text.

Website Extra!
A copy of the features and components from Activity 2 are available on the website. Cut these out and sort them into each text type – remember to add your own ones too.

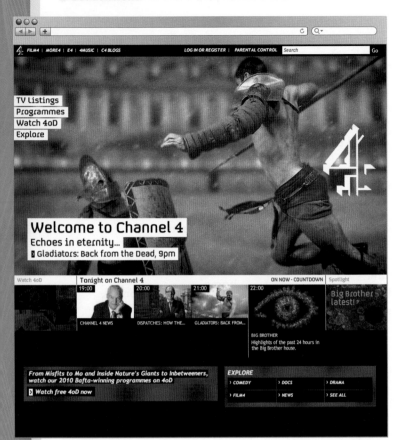

Welcome to Channel 4
Echoes in eternity…
Gladiators: Back from the Dead, 9pm

Website

http://www.channel4.com

Blog

This week in *The Cut*, Tim Henman chats to us about his picks for Wimbledon 2010, Tim Robey checks out the week's new movies and Claudine Beaumont has played with the new iPhone and 3DS – but are they any good?

Podcast

Andrew Johnson Profile

Information
London
Birthday: 24th January

Need a new camera?
Click here to view our photographic equipment
CLICK HERE

+ Add as a friend

My photos
Friends / Requests
My messages 2 new messages
My privacy settings

Andrew says…
I'm bored today!

Message from Emily…
I saw the photos from your party, they're really funny!

Message from Irfan…
I've just bought a new game for my Wii. Want to come over?

Social networking

From: example@bhf.org.uk

To: example@bhf.org.uk

This would be a great way raising some funds.

Mobile communication

Digital video

Changing conventions

When choosing an appropriate digital text to write about in your examination it is important to remember that digital text conventions can change to suit the needs of the intended audience.

A good example of this is Twitter. Twitter began as a forum for exchanging messages between friends. It has now changed to include celebrity watches and updates, protest groups and even education posts by teachers. You can follow people you don't know and who don't know you.

Activity 4

1. Research how the conventions of blogging have changed to meet the needs of the audience. You could use an internet search engine, such as Google, for your research.

   You should investigate:

   - the emergence of blogging
   - the conventions of early blogs
   - how and why the conventions of blogs have changed.

Activity 5

Investigate three blogs. Refer back to your findings in Activity 4 to remind yourself of the conventions of blogs.

1. List the conventions that are common to all the blogs.

2. Are there any conventions that are specific to each blog? Copy and complete the table below to record your findings.

Blog	Subject	Conventions
A	Travel – gap year student travelling around Australia	Map – shows the route they are travelling

Preparing for your examination

When preparing for your examination:

- Identify the main conventions of the types of digital texts you might be assessed on (see page 6). This is important in both sections of the examination.

- Be prepared to discuss changing conventions in digital texts – this is especially important for Section B when you will be expected to have a wide understanding of typical and challenging conventions in relation to the digital text you have already studied.

4 Websites

This chapter will help you to...

* identify the conventions of a website

* identify the features and components of a website

* explore how the website is being used to serve an audience and a purpose

You might be asked to analyse a website in your examination. A website can be visited by anyone around the world who knows the web address or finds the website using a search engine.

The first thing you should do is identify the audience(s) and purpose(s) of the website. The audience of a website might be looking for:

* information
* education
* entertainment.

Identifying the purpose is important because it will help you to explain how the conventions of a website are used within it. The producer of the website will think carefully about the purpose of the digital text when deciding which features and components to use. As you learned in Chapter 2, features and components are used to communicate the intended messages to the audience.

Look at the home page of the World Wide Fund for Nature (WWF) website below.

The **audience** is adults who care about animals. The **purpose** of the website is to raise public awareness of the charity and encourage people to support it by donating money.

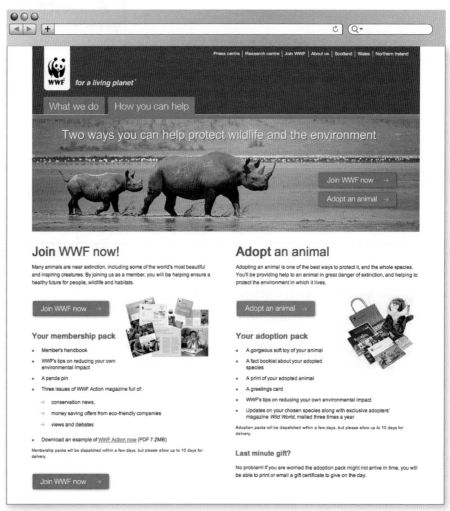

Photo: Black rhinoceros (Diceros bicornis) © Michel Terrettaz/WWF-Canon

The **components** of the website – the three 'Join WWF now' buttons, links and interactive buttons – are all designed to make it easy for the audience to feel sympathy for the cause, become a member and donate money.

The **features** support the messages of the website. The slogan 'Two ways you can help protect wildlife and the environment' is placed within the image to draw the audience's attention to the two rhinos. The image of the rhino with its baby has an impact on the audience by encouraging us to want to protect them.

Activity 1

Visit the WWF website and take a screenshot of the home page.

1   Label the screenshot with as many of the features and components of a website as you can identify. A checklist is given below.

Components	Features
Banner	Caption
Tabs	Headline
Button	Logo
Icon	Slogan
Link	Image
Hyperlink	Language features
Search bar tool	Colour
Audio	Boxes
Video	Columns

2   Explain how each feature and component is used to help the audience understand the messages of the website.

ResultsPlus
Watch out

■ In your examination you will be asked to identify the features and components separately from being asked to comment on them. You gain fewer marks for identifying than you do for commenting. Use words like 'because', 'suggest' and 'implies' when commenting on the features and components, otherwise you will only be describing what you see.

Activity 2

Visit one of the following websites: BBC News, Oxfam or Nickelodeon.

1   Identify the audience(s) and purpose(s) of your chosen website.

2   Identify three features and three components of the website.

3   How are these features and components used to impact on the website's audience and achieve the purpose?

> Headlines are used so readers can see what stories are relevant to them...
>
> News feeds grab the audience's attention and make sure they have the latest news. This makes the audience feel that the website is very up-to-date...

Channel 4 has a reputation for making challenging programmes that target a wide range of audiences. Channel 4's website aims to reflect this reputation.

Activity 3

Explore the Channel 4 website.

1. How is the home page organised? What conventions of a website does it use?

   > There are different tabs for programmes...

2. How are audiences encouraged to interact with the site (and even with Channel 4 itself)?

3. Scroll to the bottom of the site, and open the 'About 4' link. What information does this lead to?

4. Stay inside the 'About 4' link. Under the 'Useful links' tab, open the '4 Producers' link, and then click on 'Commissioning'. What does this tell you about?

5. Present or discuss what you have learned about Channel 4 from its website.

The Channel 4 website communicates the identity of the channel. It is a good website to explore to find out how the website and TV channel link intertextually.

Activity 4

Review what you have learned from the Channel 4 website.

1. Identify and comment on the features and components of the website that are used to appeal to the intended audience and achieve the website's purpose.

2. What are the strengths and weaknesses of the Channel 4 website?

3. Is the Channel 4 website successful? Think about what the website's purpose is and judge if it meets its aims.

Preparing for your examination

In preparation for your examination:

- Make sure you can identify the intended audience(s) and purpose(s) of different websites in Section A. You should practise explaining how a website's features and conventions create impact and meanings.

- You should be prepared to discuss the key components and any changing conventions that might be relevant to the audience(s) of the website in Section B.

- Make sure you are able to consider whether using a website would be appropriate to fulfil a given brief. You will need to plan which features, components and conventions, e.g. home page layout, hyperlinks, images and pop-up/banner adverts, the text will include and explain why these are effective.

ResultsPlus
Self assessment

Check your answers to the activities in this chapter.

When reading and understanding websites have you:

- identified the features and components used by the producer?
- selected specific examples from the text you are responding to?
- commented on these examples, linking to audience, purpose and messages?

5 Digital video

In your examination you might be asked to comment on a digital video, which is a video recording that has been produced on a digital camera (or has been converted to digital). Digital videos can be edited on a computer and can be embedded into other digital texts, such as a website. They can also be accessed through video libraries and websites such as YouTube. However, digital videos can also be independent from other digital texts and can be shown at the cinema or on television.

Like other digital texts, it is important to start by identifying the audience(s) and purpose(s) of the digital video. You will then be able to identify and explain how the producer has used the features and components to communicate a message to the audience.

This chapter will help you to...

* identify the conventions of a digital video
* identify the features and components of a digital video
* explore how the digital video is being used to serve an audience and a purpose

Activity 1

Watch some local news reports to familiarise yourself with their features and components. You should also revise the sections in Unit 1 on the elements of moving images, particularly film techniques and audience interpretations.

1. Working in groups of three, imagine that you have been asked to create a short news item in which you film a celebrity visiting your school and conduct an interview with them. The news bulletin will be used on your local news website.

STUDENT 1

As the **reporter** for the news item, plan the script.

* Will you use voiceover or speak direct to camera?
* You will need an introduction, some link material and a conclusion.
* What questions will you ask the celebrity?

STUDENT 2

As the **editor** for the news item, plan the footage.

* What establishing shot will you use to start the item?
* How will you film the reporter? (Remember you will need at least two 'to camera' sections.)
* What footage will you need of the celebrity?
* How will you film and edit the interview?

STUDENT 3

As the **producer** of the news item, plan the overall finish.

* What do you feel is the purpose of the news item?
* What graphic images or onscreen text might you use?
* What music or sound effects will you use to establish the 'feel' of the item?
* What do you want the overall effect on the audience to be?

In Activity 1 you planned which features and components to include in your news clip. Remember that:

- **features** are anything to do with the digital video's presentation, layout or language, such as onscreen text, the images used, the words and music in the soundtrack
- **components** are anything that relate to the functionality of the digital video, such as the soundtrack, video footage and the editing choices that have been made.

In your examination you will be asked to identify features and components, and explain how effective they are in communicating messages to the audience.

Activity 2

Watch a short film and a music video on YouTube.

1. Identify the intended audience(s) and purpose(s) of each video.

2. Identify three features and three components of each video.

3. How are these features and components used to appeal the audience and achieve the purpose of each digital video?

4. How effective are the digital videos in terms of their use of conventions, footage, editing and overall impact on the audience?

Activity 3

Website Extra!
Follow the links to watch the advertisements referred to in Activity 3.

Choose one of the digital video advertisements listed below for Sony Bravia televisions:
- **Rabbits**
- **Paint splash**
- **Bouncy balls**

1. Identify the key features of the advertisement and explain how they are used to create particular effects. Copy and complete this table to record your answers.

Feature	Effect
Piece of music by José Gonzalez	The sound of the guitar at the beginning of the song creates a calm and relaxing atmosphere...

2. What are the obvious messages about Sony Bravia for audiences on first viewing?

3. What are your expectations of a digital video advertisement for a piece of electrical equipment? What are their usual conventions? (e.g. Do they usually feature a scientist, or a couple, or impressive statistics?)

4. Look again at your chosen advertisement. How does it meet your expectations and how does it surprise you with its actual use of conventions?

In your examination you will be asked to choose appropriate digital texts to fulfil a brief. Understanding why producers create digital videos will help you with this.

Film trailers

Film trailers are very similar to advertisements as they promote a product. They are an important part of the run-up to a film's release, both at the cinema and when the DVD is released for home viewing. Trailers often have big budgets, because film studios are aware that they can generate strong interest in a film before it is released.

Activity 4

Watch at least four online film trailers.

1. Give each trailer a star award (five stars is the highest rating) to show how much you want to see the film after watching the trailer. Explain your reasons for giving each award.

2. Choose one trailer. Identify the intended audience and the strengths and weaknesses of the trailer in appealing to this audience.

3. What messages about the film will audiences pick up from the way the trailer is constructed? (Choose specific features that the trailer is using effectively.)

4. How does your chosen trailer use conventions in

   a) typical ways   **b)** surprising ways

   to appeal to audiences? (Think of conventions connected to genre, image, camera, graphics and sound. How do the conventions in the trailer meet your expectations or surprise you?)

A still from the trailer for the *Shrek Forever After* (2010) film.

 Results Plus
Build better answers

Look at this examination question:

Evaluate the effectiveness of the *Dark Knight* (2008) film trailer in promoting the film.

■ A **Band 1** answer (1-2 marks) will be **basic** and **undeveloped** with little reference to the features and components used by the film-maker. The answer might list things such as the music and close-up shots but not really say anything about them.

● A **Band 2** answer (3-4 marks) will have **clear references** to features and components and a **clear evaluation of effectiveness**. The answer might pick out the dramatic music that sounds like a quickening heartbeat and point out that this is an effective way of suggesting the film will be exciting and action-packed.

▲ A **Band 3** answer (5-6 marks) will be **original** and **imaginative**, using **effective** and **sustained references** to the text to explore **well-judged** comments on effectiveness. For example, the trailer emphasises Heath Ledger's performance as the Joker but much of the plot revolves around Batman's sense of loss. This might mislead the audience into thinking that the film is nothing more than good guy versus bad guy when it is more complicated than this.

Website Extra!
An information sheet on film trailer conventions is available on the website.

Advertisements

Digital videos that can be used in websites as pop-ups or banners, sent to mobile phones or attached to e-mails are now used in advertising. You should remember that many advertisements are created for television and are later posted online by viewers so they can comment on them.

When you examine the use of digital videos in advertising, think about the audience and purpose, the message and the conventions, and how the features and components are used to communicate these effectively to the audience.

Website Extra!
Follow the link to view the Boss Orange advertisement.

Activity 5

Watch the advertisement for Boss Orange starring Sienna Miller on YouTube. Think about the conventions the advertisement is using to create an impact on the intended audience.

1. Read this student's response to the question:

> **Evaluate the effectiveness of the video in promoting perfume.**

> In the perfume advert for Boss Orange, actress Sienna Miller is used as the central character. She is represented as a stylish, though 'hippy' girl who is fun-loving and happy. With British Beatles music in the background, she is seen applying the perfume and then posing for different shots where she is smiling, laughing, striking poses, winking, etc. The fact that the bottle looks a bit like a camera is used to help us understand that the bottle is the camera that is capturing her spirit, and that anyone else who uses the perfume will be just as happy as Sienna.
>
> The advert relies on audiences knowing that Sienna has made many popular films and has a reputation for having lots of famous boyfriends. The representation of Sienna in this advert suggests that it would not be hard for audiences to live like her!

2. Do you agree with the student's response? Give your reasons.

3. Now write your own response to evaluate how effective the advertisement is in appealing to the intended audience and serving its purpose. How effective are the conventional features and components in communicating the advertisement's message?

In recent years there has been an increase in home or industry produced digital video advertisements that use social networking sites to reach audiences and increase brand awareness. This is called **viral marketing**. Some of the most popular viral campaigns include those from Nike, Quicksilver, Dove and Diet Coke.

Reaching audiences: YouTube

Producers of digital videos also consider how audiences will view their texts. In your examination you will need to plan an appropriate digital text to fulfil a brief. If you are proposing a digital video, you should think about how audiences will access the video and why this is important.

YouTube allows users to upload and share digital videos. Many of the videos on YouTube are created by the users themselves and include short webcasts, music videos and short films.

YouTube is also used by celebrities and companies like the BBC to reach a wide audience. Viewers can rate the videos and this can have a big impact on the success of bands and film-makers – some bands have been signed to record labels because their videos have become so popular online.

> **Key Terms**
>
> **Viral marketing:** a method of marketing that encourages people to pass on the message to others.

> **Website Extra!**
> You can read more about viral marketing on the website.

Activity 6

Go to YouTube and type in the term 'Honda Civic Type R'. Click on a video that has been produced by a professional broadcaster such as the BBC. Now click on the arrow next to the number of views.

1. Who is most likely to have watched the video?

2. Look at the list of links. Where has the video been used and how has this helped to get people to watch?

3. How could Honda use this information to help them sell their cars?

Preparing for your examination

In preparation for your examination:

- Make sure you can identify the intended audience(s) and purpose(s) of digital videos for Section A. You will need to discuss how key features and conventions are being used to create impact and meanings in a digital video.

- Check you can comment on the use of components to communicate messages to the audience(s) for Section B. You will also need to evaluate how effective the digital text is in achieving its purpose.

- Make sure you are able to consider whether using a digital video would be appropriate to fulfil a given brief. You will need to plan which features, components and conventions, e.g. a home page with embedded video, a storyboard, a shooting script or an advertisement, the text will include and explain why these are effective.

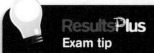

Results Plus
Exam tip

⚠ In the examination you will be asked to use digital texts to fulfil a brief you have been given. Think about how you would use digital video to advertise a product or to explore an idea for a website. What choices would you make to create a specific impact on your audience?

6 Podcasts

One of the types of digital text you might be asked to write about in the examination is a podcast. Podcasts are audio or audio-visual files which are downloaded or streamed to mobile MP3 players or personal computers. Links to podcasts are usually found on the podcast's website and are often free to download There are a huge range of podcasts for different audiences and purposes.

Although podcasts often sound like spontaneous conversation, they are likely to be scripted.

Podcasts delivered by one presenter are often like dramatic monologues, extended speeches by an individual that give us a sense of their character and situation. They follow some key conventions:

- A clear sense of character in terms of accent, words chosen and style.
- A reason for speaking – the monologue often addresses a social issue (e.g. teenage drinking), an emotion (e.g. loneliness) or a reaction to a situation (e.g. receiving exam results).
- A point of view and state of mind in relation to the issue, emotion or situation.

This chapter will help you to...

- identify the conventions of a podcast
- identify the features and components of a podcast
- explore how podcasts are being used to serve an audience and a purpose

Website Extra!

Stephen Fry's Podgrams are a good example of dramatic monologue technique. Other podcasts, like Mark Kermode and Simon Mayo's Film Reviews are like conversations. There are links to some examples of podcast styles on the website.

Activity 1

Listen to three podcasts of your choice.

1. For each podcast, make a note of the following:
   a) who the intended audience(s) of the podcast is
   b) what the purpose of the podcast is
   c) the structure of the podcast.

2. List the things the three podcasts have in common.

3. Write a list of conventions for a podcast.

4. When do you think it is appropriate to use podcasts? Are they suited to some ideas/subjects more than others?

Identifying the audience(s) and purpose(s) of a podcast will help you to explain how podcast conventions are used effectively. Producers of podcasts will think carefully about the purpose when deciding which features and components to use to communicate the intended messages to the audience.

Listen to a podcast from the Capital FM Breakfast Show. Some of the features and components are identified below.

> **Website Extra!**
> Follow the links to listen to podcasts listed on this page.

> The language used creates a sense of the presenters' voice and personality.

> The podcasts can include outside broadcasts or interviews.

> The podcast can be accessed through a home page via RSS feed or other link.

> The subject of the podcast is centred on a specific topic.

> The podcasts include a clear point of view or set of opinions.

> The podcasts contain jingles and music as well as voices (in some podcasts copyright issues mean that music choices can be restricted).

> They are an edited or shortened version /highlights of another broadcast (the Capital FM Breakfast Show).

> They are a 'zoo' format (a group discussion rather than just an individual monologue).

Activity 2

Visit the podcasts section on the BBC Radio 5 live website. Listen to the discussion in one of the Mark Kermode and Simon Mayo's Film Reviews podcasts.

1. Identify the audience(s) and purpose(s) of the podcast.

2. Identify three features and three components of the podcast.

3. How are these features and components used to appeal to the audience(s) and achieve the purpose(s) of the podcast?

4. How effective is the podcast in using podcast conventions to impact on the audience?

In your examination you will be asked to consider how different digital texts could be used to fulfil a brief. When planning a digital text to fulfil a brief, you will need to consider the context. As you learned in Chapter 2, there are many categories of text and conventions can change depending on the category of the digital text you are using.

Activity 3

1. Give three examples of how a podcast could be used effectively in a charitable context.

> A fundraiser could give a weekly update on how a charitable event is going.

2. What are the strengths and weaknesses of using a podcast to communicate effectively with audiences?

Preparing for your examination

When preparing for your examination:

- Make sure you can identify the intended audience(s) and purpose(s) of a range of podcasts for Section A. You should also be able to discuss how key features and conventions are being used to create impact and meanings.
- Practise commenting on the use of components to communicate messages to audiences in the pre-released podcast. You will also need to evaluate on how effective the text is in achieving its purpose.
- Make sure you are able to consider whether using a podcast would be appropriate to fulfil a given brief. You will need to plan which features, components and conventions, e.g. homepage, script and list of items to be covered, the text will include and explain why these are effective.

7 Blogs

In your examination you might be asked to analyse a blog. The first blogs (web logs) were originally used as a way of sharing technical information with other computer experts. They were usually just lists of links. It is only in recent years that blogging has developed into its current form. Free blog websites with 'push button' publishing, such as Blogger and Live Journal, have made it easy for anyone to publish a blog.

This chapter will help you to...

* identify the conventions of a blog
* identify the features and components of a blog
* explore how blogs are being used to serve an audience and a purpose

Activity 1

Investigate blogs by conducting a survey.

1. Ask your classmates:

   * to define a blog
   * to explain the potential benefits of blogging
   * why they think people want to blog.

Watch the clip from The Weblog Project on the website.

2. Compare your survey findings with the clip from The Weblog Project. This showcases members of the public and media professionals telling you what they think a blog is. Make a note of the similarities and differences between your survey and The Weblog Project's survey.

Website Extra!

Follow the link to The Weblog Project before you complete question 2 in Activity 1.

In the simplest terms, a blog is an online diary which provides a log of someone's thoughts, ideas, useful links, photos, videos, or the latest news. It is a way of communicating ideas, opinions and beliefs about any subject.

When analysing blogs in preparation for your examination you should begin by identifying the intended audience(s) and purpose(s). This will help you to explain how the conventions of a blog are used within it. The producer of the blog will think carefully about the audience and purpose when deciding which features and components to use to communicate the intended messages effectively.

Look at the travel blog below. Some blog conventions have been labelled for you.

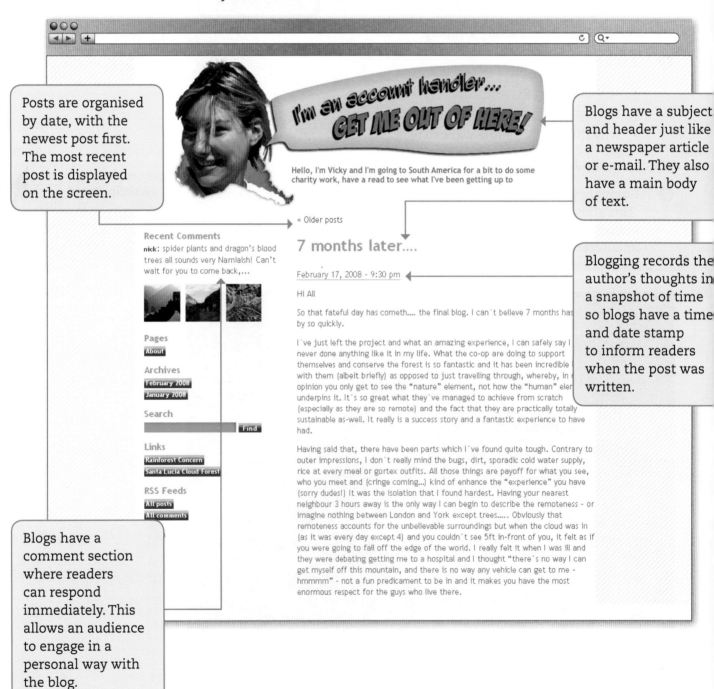

Posts are organised by date, with the newest post first. The most recent post is displayed on the screen.

Blogs have a subject and header just like a newspaper article or e-mail. They also have a main body of text.

Blogging records the author's thoughts in a snapshot of time so blogs have a time and date stamp to inform readers when the post was written.

Blogs have a comment section where readers can respond immediately. This allows an audience to engage in a personal way with the blog.

I'm an account handler... GET ME OUT OF HERE!

Hello, I'm Vicky and I'm going to South America for a bit to do some charity work, have a read to see what I've been getting up to

« Older posts

Recent Comments

nick: spider plants and dragon's blood trees all sounds very Narniaish! Can't wait for you to come back,...

Pages
About

Archives
February 2008
January 2008

Search
Find

Links
Rainforest Concern
Santa Lucia Cloud Forest

RSS Feeds
All posts
All comments

7 months later....

February 17, 2008 - 9:30 pm

Hi All

So that fateful day has cometh.... the final blog. I can't believe 7 months has by so quickly.

I've just left the project and what an amazing experience, I can safely say I never done anything like it in my life. What the co-op are doing to support themselves and conserve the forest is so fantastic and it has been incredible with them (albeit briefly) as opposed to just travelling through, whereby, in opinion you only get to see the "nature" element, not how the "human" ele underpins it. It's so great what they've managed to achieve from scratch (especially as they are so remote) and the fact that they are practically totally sustainable as-well. It really is a success story and a fantastic experience to have had.

Having said that, there have been parts which I've found quite tough. Contrary to outer impressions, I don't really mind the bugs, dirt, sporadic cold water supply, rice at every meal or gortex outfits. All those things are payoff for what you see, who you meet and (cringe coming...) kind of enhance the "experience" you have (sorry dudes!) It was the isolation that I found hardest. Having your nearest neighbour 3 hours away is the only way I can begin to describe the remoteness – or imagine nothing between London and York except trees..... Obviously that remoteness accounts for the unbelievable surroundings but when the cloud was in (as it was every day except 4) and you couldn't see 5ft in-front of you, it felt as if you were going to fall off the edge of the world. I really felt it when I was ill and they were debating getting me to a hospital and I thought "there's no way I can get myself off this mountain, and there is no way any vehicle can get to me – hmmmm" – not a fun predicament to be in and it makes you have the most enormous respect for the guys who live there.

Activity 2

Look at this blog and research some other examples.

BLOGS HOME » CULTURE » HARRY MOUNT

Harry Mount

Harry Mount is the author of Amo, Amas, Amat and All That: How to Become a Latin Lover and A Lust for Windowsills - a Guide to British Buildings from Portcullis to Pebbledash. A former leader writer for the Telegraph, he writes about politics, buildings and language for lots of British and American newspapers and magazines.

Why do Englishmen dress so badly in the heat?

By **Harry Mount** | Last updated: July 11th, 2010

60 Comments | Comment on this article

David Niven demonstrates correct dress for the summer

Recent Posts

Weddings have become conspicuous consumption egofests
July 13th, 2010 13:22
1 Comment

The death of the bath: another casualty of the pace of modern life
July 12th, 2010 15:31
22 Comments

Martin Amis: it makes sense that he's a feminist
July 12th, 2010 11:45
11 Comments

Raoul Moat: the police did their best to save his life
July 12th, 2010 8:57
27 Comments

Why do Englishmen dress so badly in the heat?
July 11th, 2010 10:22
60 Comments

1. Identify the audience(s) and pupose(s) of the blog(s).

2. In pairs make a list of the features you think a blog should have.

3. Now make a list of the components you think a blog should have.

4. Note down the blog conventions you have found in your examples. Make a list of any different conventions the blogs include.

Website Extra!
Do you know what the **blogosphere**, a **phlog** and a **vlog** are? Download the blogging glossary to explore some blogging key terms.

Activity 3

Look at this extract from a blog. Visit the blog online to explore it further.

Copyright Guardian News & Media Ltd 2010

1. Who is the target audience for this text? Give reasons for your answer.

2. Identify the features (layout, language and content) and the components (functionality) that the home page uses. Explain how effective these are in helping the text to appeal to its audience and achieve its purpose.

3. How are audiences encouraged to interact with the blog? What enjoyment could an audience gain from this site?

4. Now choose another blog. Grab the screen and paste it into a document. Make a list of bullet points about the blog. Consider:

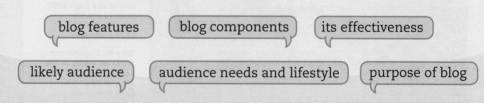

blog features   blog components   its effectiveness

likely audience   audience needs and lifestyle   purpose of blog

In your examination you will be asked to plan an appropriate digital text to fulfil a brief. If you choose to use a blog, you should consider the reasons why people blog. Remind yourself of the list you created in Activity 1. Your classmates might have suggested a wide range of reasons, such as sharing your thoughts with a wider audience.

Activity 4

Discuss with your classmates the benefits of having a blog.

1 Make a list of the benefits of setting up blogging pages under these headings:

- recognition
- employment opportunities
- to make money

For businesses there are a lot of benefits to blogging. Search engines tend to find more easily websites that are updated regularly, and place them higher in search results. Blogging is a good way to make sure that your content is always new, and therefore regularly checked by search engines like Google.

Another way to gain recognition for a blog is by labelling the entries with frequently used search terms so that they are seen by the right people.

Activity 5

Imagine that you work for a company that wants to encourage young people to travel in their gap year (usually an extended holiday taken between school and university).

1 How might blogs be a useful tool for this task?

2 How would you make sure your blog was looked at rather than others?

3 What are the strengths and weaknesses of using blogs for this purpose?

ResultsPlus
Watch out

Don't fall into the trap of believing that an idea is silly or inappropriate just because you don't like it – you are probably not the intended audience for the text. Put yourself in the position of the intended audience before making comments about strengths and weaknesses.

Some blogging has become very influential in news reporting. This online journalism is different from the traditional reporting in a newspaper and the blogger might have more freedom and independence.

Blogs are harder to control than broadcast or print-based media, so they can be used to raise awareness about social and political injustice. In some countries bloggers have criticised a government or politicians and faced imprisonment.

Activity 6

To help you revise the key ideas relating to blogs, choose one of the tasks below and plan a blog.

> **A** A blog about your pet intended for members of your family who no longer live at home.

> **B** A political blog aimed at voters to persuade them to think carefully before voting.

> **C** A blog about cars aiming to keep enthusiasts informed on the latest advances.

1 How will the audience influence your choice of content and language for your blog?

2 Use what you have learned about blog conventions, features and components in this chapter to plan your blog page.

Activity 7

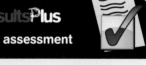

ResultsPlus

Self assessment

Check your answer to **Activity 7**. Have you:
- developed your response, considering what will be original and imaginative?
- considered the specific features and components that you would use?
- commented on how these features and components will be effective?

Review your plan from Activity 6.

1 Create a PowerPoint presentation explaining the choices you have made and how effective you think your blog is in communicating its message.

2 Ask other members of your class for feedback.

Preparing for your examination

When preparing for your examination:

- Make sure you can identify the intended audience(s) and purpose(s) of a range of blogs for Section A. You should also be able to discuss how key features and conventions are being used to create impact and meanings.
- Practise commenting on the use of components to communicate messages to audiences in the pre-released blog. You will also need to evaluate how effective the blog is in achieving its purpose.
- Make sure you are able to analyse whether using a blog would be appropriate to fulfil a given brief. You will need to plan which features, components and conventions, e.g. home page, opening paragraph, description of key issues being covered, the text will include and explain why these are effective.

8 Social networking and mobile communication

In your examination you might be asked to analyse a page from a social networking and mobile communication.

Social networking

A social network is a group of individuals (or organisations) connected by a common interest, friendship, belief or some other type of relationship. Sites like Facebook, MySpace and Twitter allow individual members to communicate with each other and help businesses reach wider audiences to promote their products.

Activity 1

Design a questionnaire about social networking sites.

1. Use the questionnaire to find out:
   a) which social networking sites people in your class use. Ask your teachers as well as other pupils. Are some sites more popular than others?
   b) why people use social networking sites (e.g. to play games, keep in touch with distant friends or relatives, chat to school friends, meet like-minded people, etc.).

2. Make a list of the most popular reasons.

Below is an example of the components of a social networking site.

Your personal details can be made public or private.

Bespoke adverts appear alongside your profile page.

A profile picture enables you to customise your page.

Your profile page has links to your details, photos, etc.

Alert buttons show you when you have friend requests, messages and notifications.

Andrew Johnson Profile

Information   Hide/Show
London
Birthday: 24th January

Need a new camera?
Click here to view our photographic equipment
CLICK HERE

+ **Add as a friend**

My photos

Friends / Requests

My messages 2 new messages

My privacy settings

Andrew says...
I'm bored today!

Message from Emily...
I saw the photos from your party, they're really funny!

Message from Irfan...
I've just bought a new game for my Wii. Want to come over?

Your status is displayed on your wall and your friends can leave messages and comments for you here.

Activity 2

Study the screenshots of social networking sites available on the companion website.

1. Identify the audience(s) and purpose(s) of the sites.
2. Identify three features of the sites.
3. Consider the components in the table below and see if they are used on each site. Add any other components that you think are missing.

Component	Site 1	Site 2	Site 3
Home page			
Live instant chat			
Video and photo upload			
Personal profile			
Status updates			
Displayed personal details and key dates			
Friends			
Personal and public messaging			
Games			
Different modes of access			
Links to friends (suggestions and accept/decline)			
Bespoke advertising			
News feeds			
Groups			

4. How do these components appeal to the audience and achieve the purpose of the sites?

Website Extra!
Download the Twitter case study to find out more.

Twitter is a social networking site on which users exchange quick messages to keep people up to date about the things that happen in between e-mails and blog posts. These updates ('tweets') are displayed on a user's home page or can be sent to the user's 'followers'. Twitter posts can be updated using the Twitter website, a mobile phone or instant messages.

Businesses and social networking

As many people use the internet to search for product information, an online presence is essential for businesses. Many businesses use social networking sites alongside, or instead of, traditional marketing and promotional methods.

The advantages of this are:

- The business can build a profile and update content regularly.
- They can advertise weekly or monthly offers as well as giving general information about the company/business.

- It is free; for MySpace, Facebook and Twitter you only need a valid e-mail address to create a page, whereas traditional marketing methods usually have to be paid for.

- Businesses are able to target the right customers by using bespoke advertisements (see Chapter 1, page 56).

- It is more environmentally friendly as the advertisements are electronic and do not use printed materials.

Jewellery company Silversaurus is an example of a company that uses a Facebook page to promote its business. It also has a website where people can find out about the company and order goods.

Activity 3

1. How could a charity, a new band and a small independent retailer use social networking sites?

2. What are the strengths and weaknesses of using social networking sites in this way?

> The company can regularly update customers with news...
>
> Some people might write negative comments...

Mobile communication

E-mail is a valuable communication tool that allows companies to reach a large number of people very quickly at a low cost. This is particularly useful for non-profit organisations and charities, which can reach potential donors, send them news alerts, invitations and thank-you messages. The addresses come from people who have asked to be on a mailing list or from lists of e-mail addresses sold on by direct mail companies.

Activity 4

1. Look at one of your personal e-mails and list the features.

2. Make a note of any features you would change if sending the same e-mail for business purposes.

3. Make a list of different e-mail categories (e.g. personal e-mails between friends).

4. Copy and complete the table below to record the conventions for the different e-mail categories you listed.

E-mail category	Conventions
Personal e-mails	Informal language and slang, fun slogan as part of e-mail signature...

Here is an example of an e-mail that the British Heart Foundation (BHF) sent out to promote awareness and encourage fundraising.

| From: example@bhf.org.uk | Date: Thu, 8 Apr 2010 16:05:14 +0100 |
| To: example@bhf.org.uk | Subject: Cardiff Fun Run |

Llanishen Rotary Club is organising a fun run in Bute Park on Sunday 23rd May.
This would be a great way for people to support the Cardiff Heart Nurse Appeal by taking part and raising some funds.

I attach a poster with full details and would be grateful if you would circulate to everyone you know who may be interested, and also if you can display the poster at work or anywhere else suitable I would be grateful.

As you will see we will be giving our supporters a free BHF running vest to wear with pride on the day.

Many thanks for your help.

Kimberly

Let us help you live with a healthy heart

Heart Matters is the FREE service from the BHF that gives you personalised information on how to look after your heart health. Sign up today and you'll enjoy regular issues of heart matters magazine, access to our friendly HelpLine, an online lifestyle check and much more. To find out more visit www.bhf.org.uk/heart or call 0300 330 3300.

Kimberly Gower Fundraising Volunteer Manager British Heart Foundation

Activity 5

Look at the BHF e-mail above.

1. Identify the audience(s) and purpose(s) of the e-mail.

2. Identify three features of this e-mail.

3. Look closely at the language (which is a feature) of the e-mail. How has the author used language to serve the charity's needs? (For example, use of the slogan, vocabulary used.)

4. How effective is this e-mail as a way of raising funds and interesting new clients?

Preparation for your examination

When preparing for your examination:

- Make sure you can identify the intended audience(s) and purpose(s) of a range of social networking sites and mobile communication for Section A. You should also be able to discuss how key features and conventions are being used to create impact and meanings.

- Practise commenting on the use of components to communicate messages to audiences. You will also need to evaluate how effective social networking sites and mobile communication are in achieving their purpose.

- Make sure you are able to analyse whether using a social networking site and mobile communication would be appropriate to fulfil a given brief. You will need to plan which features, components and conventions, e.g. home page, embedded advertisements, realistic messages, forums, the text will include and explain why these are effective.

In your examination you will be asked to plan a digital text to fulfil a brief. In Section A you will be asked to select a digital text and explain which features you would choose to fulfil the brief. In Section B you will be asked to select a number of digital texts that can work together to build a strategy to fulfil the brief.

Look at this example of a question from Section A of your examination:

Julie Webster would like to keep a record of her children as they grow up. She would like to do this in an imaginative way. She is considering using **one** of the following digital texts:

- social networking site

- blog

- website

Choose the digital text you would advise Julie Webster to use. For this digital text you must:

- describe the features you would use

- explain why these features would be effective.

Activity 1

Read the examination question above.

1. Choose the digital text you would advise Julie Webster to use and briefly explain your choice.

2. Copy and complete the table below. Describe the features you would include in your digital text and explain the strengths and weaknesses of using each one. One row has been completed for you as an example.

Feature	Description	Strengths and weaknesses of chosen feature
Images – photographs	Photos of family taken at different events with captions for each, organised into a slide show.	Strength — will create visual story of important events in the children's lives and will keep memories alive. Weakness — not very imaginative unless you could have more description in the captions under each photo.

3. Using the information you have collected in the table, write a response to the examination question. You should spend no longer than 20 minutes on this. You should use each row of the table as one paragraph in your response. You might want to use diagrams to help you.

In Section B of your examination you will need to think carefully about how digital texts can work together to create a strategy that will fulfil a brief. When planning which digital texts to use, you should consider the category of digital text in the brief. The conventions of a digital text can change depending on the category, or context, of the text.

Activity 2

There are different categories of digital texts, including:

- business purposes (e.g. retail, travel, advertising)
- charity
- personal uses (user-generated content)
- public information (e.g. a council website)
- politics (e.g. news and current affairs)
- education
- leisure and entertainment

1. Copy and complete the table below by giving an example of how each of the six digital texts in the table could be used effectively in each of the categories listed above.

	Business	Charity	Personal	Public	Politics	Education	Entertainment
Websites	Pop-ups to advertise a product on the home page	Donation page					
Digital video							
Podcasts							
Blogs							
Social networking							
Mobile communications							

2. Choose one of your examples from each category in the table above, and complete a copy of the table below to explain why the digital text is appropriate, how it would be used and what audience you intend to reach. The example below focuses on using a website for charity.

Digital text	Reasons why appropriate	How it would be used	What audience reached
Website – donation page	• Allows people quick and easy access to the charity. • Able to find out information about making a donation quickly.	• Allow donations to be made.	• People who want to become involved with local charities.

Look at this example of a question from Section B of your examination:

A new band aimed at a mass teenage audience wants to take advantage of digital texts to spread the word about their music.

Explain how the band could effectively use digital texts to promote their music. You should:

*   choose appropriate digital texts

*   choose appropriate components

*   explain how your choices would achieve the band's ambition.

Activity 3

Read the examination question above. The category of text is for business purposes as the brief is to advertise a new band.

1   Using the information you gathered in the tables in Activity 2 and the sample examination question given above, write three more examination questions that could appear in your examination paper. Remember to check that your briefs contain an audience and purpose.

2   Using the notes you have made, write a response to one of the examination questions you have written. Remember to:

*   choose appropriate digital texts

*   choose appropriate components

*   explain how your choices would be effective.

You should spend no longer than 30 minutes on this. You might want to write at least one paragraph per bullet point in your response.

Examination Practice

How will I be assessed?

You will be assessed in an examination, which will last for **1 hour and 45 minutes**. This unit is worth 40% of your final mark. The examination is divided into two sections:

> **Section A: Unseen digital texts** – you will be asked questions about two digital texts you have not studied before. You will be asked questions about the audience and purpose of the text, the features that make up the text and how effective they are. You will also be asked to choose what digital text you would advise someone to use to fulfil a brief and explain the reasons for your choice.
>
> **Section B: Pre-released text** – you will be given six texts to study before the examination and you will be asked questions about one of these texts in the examination. You will be asked questions about the components, how the text achieves its aims, and the strengths and weaknesses of the text. You will be asked to choose what digital texts could be used effectively to fulfil a brief and explain your choices.

What am I being assessed on?

There are two assessment objectives for this unit:

AO1 Read and understand digital communication in a range of contexts selecting relevant textual detail appropriate to purpose – this is asking you to select details from the text and comment on their audience, purpose and meaning. You will be asked to select particular features or components from the text and comment on their use. You should make sure you select small details from the text and not talk about the whole text generally.

AO2 Analyse and evaluate how digital communication is designed to achieve effects and to engage and influence the audience/reader – this is asking you to comment on the strengths and weaknesses of a text or an idea you are proposing. You still need to comment on specific examples, selecting small details from the text to comment on. You need to link your analysis to the audience and purpose of the text.

How can I succeed in this assessment?

To succeed in the assessment you need to:

✓ answer the question – to do this effectively you should use words from the question in your answer

✓ plan your time – look carefully at the number of marks allocated for each question and make sure you spend an appropriate amount of time on each question

✓ answer all of the questions – do not leave any part of the paper blank.

In the examination you will be given a question paper and a resource booklet, which contains the digital texts referred to in the questions.

Sample examination paper

SECTION A: UNSEEN DIGITAL TEXTS

The questions which follow are on music.

Look at Text A (a page from the Don't Stop Believing website) in the Resource Booklet and answer the questions that follow.

1   (a) Identify **two** purposes of Text A.   (2)

     (b) Explain how the writer has achieved the purposes of Text A.   (4)

          (Total for Question 1 = 6 marks)

> These questions will always be about either audience or purpose. A good answer will show a developed understanding of the text. You can do this by saying a little bit about two different audiences or purposes, or saying a lot about one idea that you think is important.

2   (a) Identify **three** features used on the page from the Don't Stop Believing website. (3)

     (b) Explain the impact of these three features.   (9)

          (Total for Question 2 = 12 marks)

> The word 'feature' refers to the presentation of ideas. This could be the language, presentation or use of image by the writer.

Look at Text B (DJ Wolf Twitter page) in the Resource Booklet and answer the questions that follow.

3   Evaluate the effectiveness of Text B in promoting new music.   (6)

          (Total for Question 3 = 6 marks)

> You are being asked to consider how the choice of digital texts is intended to impact on the audience. For example, a website is meant to be easily accessible at all times, a digital video delivers a powerful message to a passive audience and a podcast often appeals to a specialist audience.

4   DJ Wolf is trying to attract the attention of fans who regularly go to gigs and is considering using **one** of the following digital texts:

- social networking site
- email
- podcast

Choose the digital text you would advise DJ Wolf to use.

For this digital text you must:

- describe the features you would use
- explain why these features would be effective   (10)

          (Total for Question 4 = 10 marks)

> This question will always talk about the second unseen text. It will ask you to explore the suitability of the features for the audience and purpose in the text. You should ensure that you write about the strengths and weaknesses of the text.

> Any of the different texts suggested would be suitable for the brief. You must choose one, describe the features and explain how the features will meet the audience and purpose provided.

Turn the page to see the resource booklet for Section A.

Sample resource booklet

Section A: Unseen digital texts

Text A

Text B

Sample examination paper

SECTION B: PRE-RELEASED DIGITAL TEXT

The questions that follow are on the *Guardian* podcast which you will have studied.

A transcript for this podcast has been reproduced for this pre-release text and is printed in Section B of the Resource Booklet. This is to remind you of the podcast, but you should refer to the whole *Guardian* podcast in your answers.

> You will find a reminder of this text in the resource booklet. You should write about the whole of the text based on your memory of what you have covered in class.

5 (a) Identify **three** components that show this text is a podcast. (3)

(b) Explain how the *Guardian* podcast uses these components. (9)

(Total for Question 5 = 12 marks)

> The word 'component' means the functionality of the text. This means those elements that make the text work, such as the mix of sounds in a podcast or the merging of camera shots, sound, editing techniques and onscreen text in a digital video.

6 Explain how using a podcast helps music journalists, such as those from the *Guardian*, achieve their aims. (10)

(Total for Question 6 = 10 marks)

*7 Evaluate the effectiveness of the *Guardian* podcast.

> This asterix means that you will be marked on the accuracy with which you write. You need to pay special attention to your use of sentences and spelling.

You should comment on the strengths and weaknesses of the following in your answer:

- how the aims of the podcast are achieved
- the means by which people receive the podcast
- the components and how they combine
- any other aspects you wish to consider

Use evidence from the whole text to support your answer. (10)

(Total for Question 7 = 10 marks)

> It is easy to get carried away with describing the strategy that you would use. However, it is important to describe the combination of digital texts that you think will work and consider why using these texts will be effective.

*8 A new band aimed at a mass teenage audience wants to take advantage of digital texts to spread the word about their music.

Explain how the band could effectively use digital texts to promote their music.

You should:

- choose appropriate digital texts
- choose appropriate components
- explain how your choices would achieve the band's ambition (14)

(Total for Question 8 = 14 marks)

> This question is worth the most marks on the paper. Make sure you leave enough time to complete this question. Also, make sure you leave enough time to check your answers through for the whole paper!

Sample resource booklet

SECTION B: Pre-released digital text

Text C - Transcript of *Guardian* podcast

[MUSIC]

Welcome to Music Weekly and kind regards of the season to you all. I'm Paul MacInnes and on this special last edition of the noughties, it's just music, music, music as we play our favourite live tracks from the past twelve months of pods. Upcoming we've got a whole barrage of live tracks including music from Ellie Goulding, Hockey and Mumford and Sons but we'll start the way we mean to go on with a little number from Graham Coxon. Here's an acoustic version of Sorrow's Army recorded exclusively for us.

[SONG]

That was Sorrow's Army by Graham Coxon. He didn't have a bad two thousand and nine all in all. There's no Rosie Swash in the pod with me today. She's off, probably on a jet ski, knowing her, trying to break some kind of record or other. Ellie Goulding holds the record, yes, segue there, for most appearances on 'ones to watch in two thousand and ten' lists, and we had her in the pod at the end of November. She left a distinctive spoor though and it's this version of her track Guns and Horses.

[SONG]

Ellie Goulding Guns and Horses, all you need to invade Belgium. Hockey next. They're from Portland, USA, the alfalfa sandwich capital of the world, and their brand of rock and pop is surely the product of a diet rich in vitamin K. It's their distinctly upbeat song, Song Away.

[SONG]

That was Hockey with Song Away, and as they say, tomorrow is only a song away, especially when that song is a forty minute cosmic disco rerun. A man not entirely unfamiliar with the whole disco oeuvre and a whole boxful of other oeuvres is pop polymath Patrick Wolf. He released the latest album The Bachelor to much acclaim around these parts, and so that we didn't forget what it's called he kindly played an acoustic version of the title track for us, so here it is, The Bachelor.

[SONG]

That's Patrick Wolf, The Bachelor, and a highly eligible one at that too. Now I imagine he spends ages in the bathroom.

[MUSIC 5 SECONDS]

We've got lots more great live music to come including tracks from Frightened Rabbit and Mumford and Sons, but first we don't have nearly enough artists from countries other than our own on this pod, well our own and the US which used to be our own until that unfortunate war, so it was great to have Senegalese guitarist and percussionist Baaba Maal in the studio. Here he is performing a song from his latest album, Television. This is Tindo.

[SONG]

Baaba Maal there with a rather beautiful Tindo. From one fine number to another. Frightened Rabbit, as you might guess from the name, did not make industrial noise rock. They do make fabulously delicate indie folk though and here they are with a song from their up and coming album. This is called Swim Until You Can't See The Land.

Here are some student answers to questions 2 and 8 in the examination paper on pages 89 and 92. Read the answers and the examiner comments to help you understand what you need to do to gain a good mark.

> **2** (a) Identify three features used on the page from the Don't Stop Believing website (3)
>
> (b) Explain the impact of these three features. (9)
>
> (Total for Question 2 = 12 marks)

Student 1 – Extract typical of a grade C answer

Each of these answers are correct but are they the most effective features to select? The comments that can be made about these features might not necessarily be of a high level.

There are relevant comments on the features with some reference to the audience.

2 (a) Headings

Pictures

Columns

2 (b) The headings are used to separate the text and make it easy for the audience to find the information they are interested in – nobody wants to read the whole of the website. This is why it is in columns too as it means that the page is easy to read. The pictures show what the website is about like the images of the acts in the programme.

This is a weak comment and shows that columns are perhaps not the best feature to pick out.

Examiner summary

This part of the answer is typical of grade C performance. The features selected are correct but offer little to comment on in 2b. As such, the comments in 2b are relevant but lack detail. To improve this answer, the student needs to include a lot more detail about the impact of the chosen features.

Student 2 – Extract typical of a grade A answer

The student has chosen good examples that can be explored in depth in part b.

2 (a) Bright colours

Logo

Graphics

2 (b) The aim of the bright colours and logo is to create a corporate image that is recognisable to the audience. The audience needs to be persuaded that this is the official website of the programme and this effective use of colour and logo does this. The colours chosen are powerful and are fitting for a teenage audience who would want a vibrant image. The graphics emphasise the personalities involved in the show to support the programme. They want people to get to know these people so they will continue to watch.

The level of detail in this answer is excellent and there are continuous references made to the text.

Examiner summary

This part of the answer is typical of grade A performance. This is a detailed response that effectively uses specific examples from the website to support the points the student is making. The student made sure they selected features that would offer intelligent points.

*8 A new band aimed at a mass teenage audience wants to take advantage of digital texts to spread the word about their music.

Explain how the band could effectively use digital texts to promote their music.

You should:
- choose appropriate digital texts
- choose appropriate components
- explain how your choices would achieve the band's ambition (14)

(Total for Question 8 = 14 marks)

Student 1 – Extract typical of a grade C answer

The first choice I would make is to set up a Facebook group for the band. I would include an image on the page and I would update the status with the band's latest dates and links to their music and videos. This is the place that most of their audience would go and an effective image would mean that people would get a good look at them. The links to their music and video could then be posted on the news pages of whoever is a member of their group meaning their fans can get updates.

This is a clear evaluation of the effectiveness of the page.

The student is beginning to develop the answer here.

Examiner summary

This part of the answer is typical of grade C performance. The student has chosen a digital text that clearly addresses the question and this has been developed to some degree. The answer includes some evaluation of the idea and some reference to components, but the impact of these could be explored in more depth.

Student 2 – Extract typical of a grade A answer

This is an imaginative opening to the paragraph – focusing on the way digital texts can help the band overall.

The greatest strength of digital texts is the ability to stimulate word of mouth publicity. Therefore, creating a page on a social networking site could be an effective strategy for the band. The band would need to complete the information pages and then send an invitation to as many people as possible. The more friends they attract on a page like Facebook the more people will be invited to be their friends. The band could increase the effectiveness of their Facebook page by including videos and sound files promoting their music. They could also include a link to somewhere where people could buy their music. The issue with this strategy is it relies on people being curious and looking at the page. The audience would have to be proactive and as the band is relatively unknown the audience are not likely to seek out their page.

This is a well-judged evaluation of effectiveness – noting the strengths and weaknesses of the idea.

Examiner summary

This part of the answer is typical of grade A performance. It is a detailed response that includes continuous references to the components in the chosen digital text. Throughout the answer, the evaluation is well-judged.

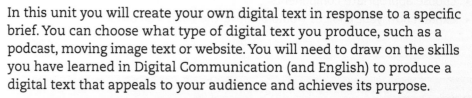

Unit 3 Creating a digital text

In this unit you will create your own digital text in response to a specific brief. You can choose what type of digital text you produce, such as a podcast, moving image text or website. You will need to draw on the skills you have learned in Digital Communication (and English) to produce a digital text that appeals to your audience and achieves its purpose.

You will work through a number of stages:

- explore the brief to find out exactly what is needed
- research the target audience and existing digital texts of a similar type
- plan a proposal
- capture (select or create) the components you need
- produce and edit your digital text
- review your work.

Your assessment

Unit 3 is a controlled assessment unit, in which you will create a digital text to fit a specific brief. Following your preparation:

- you will have up to **20 hours** to produce your final digital text and written work
- you can write up to **800 words** in total (500 words in Section A and 300 words in Section B).

The task is in three parts:

Section A: Proposal – you will need to research similar texts and use this information to write a proposal for your own digital text (up to 500 words).

Section B: Communicating through your text to your audience – you will need to produce a digital text that meets the brief and communicates its message to the target audience. You will also be assessed on your technical skill in creating your digital text.

Section C: Reviewing your text – you need to explain the choices you made when creating your digital text and explore audience feedback (up to 300 words).

Assessment Objectives

Your Unit 3 controlled assessment response will be marked using these Assessment Objectives:

AO2 Analyse and evaluate how digital communication is designed to achieve effects and to engage and influence the audience/reader.

AO3 Create digital communication, producing, adapting and using material to suit purpose and audience/reader.

1 Exploring the brief

In your controlled assessment task you will need to look carefully at the **brief** to understand exactly what it is asking you to do. First you need to identify the audience, purpose and subject matter given in the brief.

Look at this example:

> Create a digital text aimed at Year 7 secondary school students providing them with an introductory guide to your school.

| Purpose | Subject matter | Audience |

Key Term

Brief: a set of instructions for a task, project, investigation, etc.

Activity 1

In pairs or small groups, look at these three examples of briefs.

> A   Create a digital text encouraging adults to have a more positive attitude towards teenagers.

> B   Create a digital text informing children of a recent event in the news that affects their lives.

> C   Create a digital text promoting a new film for teenagers.

1   Look at each brief in turn. Identify the instructions it gives about:

a) audience – who it is for

b) purpose – what it is for

c) subject matter – what it is about.

Be prepared to share your ideas with the class.

2   For each brief, discuss with a partner:

a) what type of digital text would be most appropriate

b) what choices (e.g. layout, images, content, tone) you would need to make to ensure it was appropriate for the audience

c) what you would need to consider to ensure that the text achieved its purpose (e.g. language choices).

3   Using ideas from your discussions, decide which brief appeals to you most. What type of digital text would you produce to meet this brief?

ResultsPlus
Controlled assessment tip

⚠ However attractive and interesting you make your digital text, you will not gain high marks if you have not first identified the audience, purpose and subject matter in the brief and created your text to suit these things.

Activity 2

Look at the digital text below. It is part of an online interactive educational game.

① Write the brief that might have been given to the producer of the text. It should specify the purpose, audience and subject matter of the text.

② Explain the brief you have written. Pick out specific choices that were made by the producer of the text that helped you to identify what the brief might have said.

Audience

Identifying and understanding your audience is important. Once you have done this you can choose the most suitable language, presentation and approach for that audience.

Look again at this brief:

> **Create a digital text encouraging adults to have a more positive attitude towards teenagers.**

- Which age group would this mostly appeal to?
- What type of language would it need to use?
- What sort of presentation and approach would be most suitable?

Activity 3

Look at the home page for the Duke of Edinburgh's Award scheme below. Read the comments which identify a number of features.

1. Identify the intended audience(s) of the website.

2. Explain how each of the features identified below supports the intended audience(s).

a. Clear titles and sub-headings.

b. Images of young adults taking part.

c. Simple colour choices.

e. Appealing choice of language in introduction: 'memorable', 'rewarding'.

d. Small amount of text on home page.

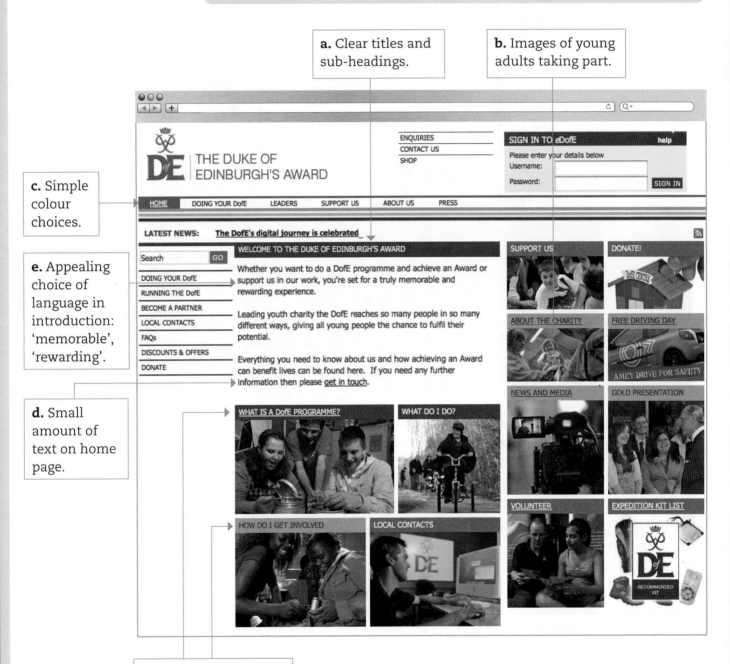

f. Rhetorical questions.

Language is an important tool that producers of digital texts use to appeal to the audience.

Read the extract below from Headliners, a children's news website. The article was written by a 15-year-old student, discussing a government proposal to raise the school leaving age to 18.

Leaving it too late

New laws are coming into place that will see the school leaving age raised to 18. Charlotte Gray, 15, looks at why the Government are doing this and speaks to other young people to get their views on the changes.

November 2007 saw the Government announce proposals to increase the school leaving age from 16 to 18. If this becomes law, it will make the new age limit 17 in 2013 and 18 from 2015.

The Government say they are doing this as young people supposedly don't have the basic skills that they require to cope in the world of work. By enforcing this law, they hope to better prepare young people to enter employment and generally make society more efficient and functional.

This law may seem like a good idea on paper. However, can young people who have decided that they don't want to stay in school after they turn 16 be physically made to stay? Katie, 15, a student in secondary education, thinks that they can and should be made to stay.

She says "It shouldn't be our decision to walk away from our GCSEs because if today's generation is not properly educated there will be no future generation of doctors and lawyers."

This article was written by Charlotte Gray, 16, for Headliners, a programme of learning through journalism for young people aged 8 to 18 www.headliners.org

1 Find examples of each of the following language features used in the article:

- facts
- alliteration
- opinions
- quotations
- rhetorical questions

2 Write two or three sentences explaining how the author's style is effective for the target audience.

Activity 5

In pairs, choose a recent news event. You could choose: freak weather conditions, a disaster such as an earthquake or volcanic eruption, or a government issue/debate/proposal, like lowering the age that teenagers can obtain a driving licence to 16.

1 Using the language features from Activity 4, write the opening of a short news article about this event, making it suitable for teenagers.

2 Repeat the exercise, this time writing the script for a news programme aimed at children aged between 8 and 12. Choose your language carefully to help your audience understand the event.

3 Write a similar news script for an adult audience. For this version, make your language more ambitious and use examples and opinions from adults.

4 Listen to each other's scripts. Which were the most effective? What made them effective?

ResultsPlus
Watch out

■ Do not create a digital text in a certain medium just because you like it. It is more important to choose a medium that is suitable for the brief. You need to explain why you chose it and why it is suitable.

Website Extra!
Copies of the tables in Activity 6 can be found on the website.

Choosing the right medium

The brief allows you to decide which **medium** of digital text to produce (for example, a podcast, moving image text or website pages). The medium you choose will depend on what the brief is asking you to do.

Look at this brief:

> Create a digital text providing Year 7 secondary school students with an introductory guide to your school.

The subject matter is your school, the target audience is new students and the purpose is to introduce them to the school. You need to decide which medium you will use to present the introductory guide.

Activity 6

Look at your controlled assessment task and think about what type of digital text you could produce in response to the brief above.

1 Complete a copy of Table 1. Evaluate the strengths and weaknesses of using each text type to meet the demands of the brief.

Table 1

Text type	Strengths	Weaknesses
Website pages		
Audio podcast or slideshow		
Moving image		

2 Now complete a copy of Table 2, suggesting what content you could include to make it appealing for your audience and to achieve the purpose of the text.

Table 2

Text type	Possible content (relating to purpose and audience)
Website pages	
Audio podcast or slideshow	
Moving image	

3 Explain which text type you think would be most appropriate and successful. Check that your ideas meet the purpose of the brief.

Accessibility

You need to consider **accessibility** when creating your digital text. Will it reach as many people as possible? Can your audience access your digital text with just a couple of clicks?

When you use the internet, you usually have some idea of what you are looking for. For example, if you want to find out about a celebrity, but do not have a specific website address, you would use a search engine. The most frequently visited websites normally appear at the top of a results page.

In your controlled assessment task, you will need to consider how your audience will access your digital text. For example, if you are planning to include your digital text on an existing website, will there be a link on the home page, or will it be located via one of the link pages?

> **Key Term**
> **Accessibility:** how easy it is for the audience to find, or 'access' a digital text

Preparing for your controlled assessment

In preparation for your controlled assessment task you should:

- Identify the audience, purpose and subject matter in your chosen brief.
- Begin to think about which medium you will use to fulfil the brief.
- Consider how your audience will access your digital text.

ResultsPlus
Controlled assessment tip

⚠ The digital text you produce must be substantial enough to be assessed. For example: one home page and four linked pages of a website; a four- to five-minute podcast; a two-minute moving image text.

2 Research

This chapter will help you to...

* research audience needs

* research existing digital texts, evaluating their conventions

You will need to follow a three-stage process when carrying out your controlled assessment task:

Section A: Proposal

* Research the target audience.

* Research digital texts of the same type as your proposed text.

* Develop a proposal for a digital text.

You can write up to 500 words in this section and it is worth 20 marks.

Section B: Communication

* Combine a variety of components including, as appropriate, moving image, still image, audio and text.

* Edit the digital text to ensure it meets the brief.

* Obtain audience feedback.

* Finalise the text so that it is suitable for its purpose and audience.

This section is worth 45 marks.

Section C: Review

* Give reasons for the choices made in creating the digital text.

* Obtain feedback from others to inform the review.

You can write up to 300 words in this section and it is worth 15 marks.

This chapter focuses on researching the target audience and researching digital texts. In your proposal you can write up to 250 words to analyse up to three digital texts you have researched, exploring the techniques used to appeal to the audience.

Research is the detailed study of something in order to find out new facts and information. The purpose of research is to increase your understanding of the audience or subject matter so you can make sure that the product you create is suitable.

Researching your target audience

You might choose to use a **focus group** when researching the needs of your intended audience. Focus groups are very useful for collecting information that can help you to make decisions. For example, the group can try out a new product and then provide feedback.

The group usually has a leader who asks **open** and **closed questions** to draw out the opinions of individuals in the group. Most focus groups have no more than ten participants.

Key Terms

Focus group: a group of people who meet to discuss their views on a subject and give feedback in response to specific questions

Open question: a question where the respondent needs to give an extended response

Closed question: a question where the respondent can answer with yes, no or a single word answer

Activity 1

In this speaking and listening activity, your teacher will ask the questions.

1. Choose ten students to take part in the focus group. The rest of the class should divide into two groups: observers and note-takers.

2. The teacher will ask the focus group six questions about a digital text, such as:

   • What is its purpose?
   • Who is the intended audience?
   • What language techniques have been used?
   • Does it achieve its purpose?
   • What components have been used?
   • How could it be improved?

3. The observers should pay close attention to the types of question the teacher asks, noticing whether they are open or closed and which are the most and least successful.

4. The note-takers should keep a record of the participants' responses.

5. When the focus group has answered all the questions, the whole class should discuss how successful the focus group was in contributing useful information. What body language was used in order to gain the responses? Did the teacher follow up on responses? If the exercise were repeated, should any of the questions be changed?

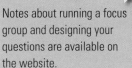

Website Extra!

Notes about running a focus group and designing your questions are available on the website.

ResultsPlus
Controlled assessment tip

⚠ In the controlled conditions, you can use your notes about the focus group and any other research you have done for your proposal, but you cannot have access to any pre-prepared digital texts.

Activity 2

Imagine that you have been provided with a brief to create a digital text about recycling aimed at teenagers. You want to use a focus group to identify what content the text should contain.

1. Make a list of questions that you could ask the focus group about what they want to know about this subject and how they would like the information to be presented. Remember to use open questions to gain detailed responses.

2. Ask a partner to look at your questions and think about how people might answer them. Work together to check that your questions will produce useful information that will help you plan your response to the brief.

You can use the outcomes of any focus groups to help you write your proposal for your digital text. In your controlled assessment proposal, part of your mark will be based on carrying out relevant research and explaining how this has contributed to your proposal.

Look at this extract from a student's proposal, explaining how the focus group helped in making decisions:

> ... I found that by collecting and discussing ideas about the content of my planned digital text, a focus group really helped. I asked a few questions and the group came up with some really good ideas. One idea was that I should include some information about how we can recycle more in school. This led me to research what we actually do now and I was surprised to find that apart from paper recycling, there's not much else being done. So in my digital text, I want to include suggestions on how we can become more eco-friendly, by encouraging and persuading our school to do more ...

Focus group feedback will be valuable when you develop your proposal, and the process can be mentioned when you review your finished digital text.

Activity 3

Read the student extract above and look at a copy of the mark scheme, which is available on the website.

1 Which part of the mark scheme is relevant to the student extract?

Researching digital texts

Once you have understood the brief and decided what type of digital text you want to produce, you will need to research existing digital texts of a similar type. Make sure they are aimed at a similar audience to the one specified in your brief.

For example, look at the following brief:

> **Create a digital text encouraging adults to have a more positive attitude towards teenagers.**

If you chose to make a podcast in response to this brief, you would need to find existing podcasts and explore them in detail, considering:

- what techniques they use to achieve their purpose
- what features they include to appeal to the intended audience
- what the **conventions** of this text type are
- how language is used to make the text effective.

Results Plus
Build better answers

Look at this controlled assessment task:

Create a digital text encouraging adults to have a more positive attitude towards teenagers.

■ A **Band 1** answer (1-5 marks) will show **limited relevant research** and there will be **limited analysis** of these texts.

● A **Band 2** answer (6-10 marks) will show **some relevant research** and there will be **some evidence** of analysis of these texts that **may inform** the decisions made in your text.

▲ A **Band 4** answer (16-20 marks) will include **focused and selective research**, with analysis that **critically informs** the decisions made in your text.

Key Term

Conventions: operating rules which apply in particular text types and aid audience recognition and understanding

Use the reading skills you developed in Unit 2 to look at the features and components of digital texts and assess how the texts are suitable for the audience and purpose, and convey the intended messages. When you find a digital text to explore, it can be useful to print out screenshots and annotate the text, identifying the key choices that the writer made.

Good places to start looking for existing digital texts are popular websites such as the *Guardian*, BBC, Channel 4 and the *Telegraph*.

Website Extra!
You can follow the links to the websites mentioned on this page.

Activity 4

Visit the *Guardian* website.

1 Find two different examples of each of the following types of digital text: a podcast, a blog and a digital video or moving image.

2 For each text you found, make notes about:

a) the route you took to find it

b) what type of digital text it is

c) its purpose

d) what it is about

e) its intended audience

f) your opinion of it.

You can use a search engine such as Google to find examples of digital texts on the subject of your brief. For example, if you search for 'attitudes towards teenagers' one of the results you get is the report below from the Sky News website. By rephrasing your search, you can often find more examples. Googling 'perception of teenagers' gives you many more results, including the page below from the *Independent* website, which would provide valuable ideas for your own digital text.

Surgeon's Shock Tactics Curb Teen Drinking

Showing school children graphic images of the 'horrific' facial injuries sustained by binge drinkers has a lasting impact on teenagers' attitude to alcohol.

According to research seen exclusively by Sky News, the 15-minute slideshow, which is given by a surgeon, can cut children's alcohol consumption by a third.
The images include a 17-year-old girl who fell and split open her nose and lost two teeth. Another shows a 15-year-old boy who had his nose bitten off in a pub.

Sky News

Behind the stereotypes: The shocking truth about teenagers

As another report complains about Britain's children, a generation is being stigmatised as promiscuous, unhealthy and violent. But are we being unfair, giving teenagers a hard time for no real reason?

The Independent Behind the stereotypes: The shocking truth about teenagers, Robert Verkaik and Arifa Akba, The Independent 23/10/2006

Key Term

Components: those elements that make a digital text work, e.g. links, home pages, icons, moving images

Explore the examples of digital texts you find in detail and look closely at the choices the writer has made. How do they help the digital text to appeal to the audience and achieve its purpose? You should also consider what **components** are used and how the digital text is put together.

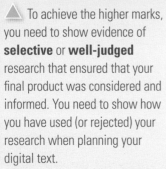

ResultsPlus
Controlled assessment tip

▲ To achieve the higher marks, you need to show evidence of **selective** or **well-judged** research that ensured that your final product was considered and informed. You need to show how you have used (or rejected) your research when planning your digital text.

When looking at the research ask yourself: does this help me with my planning? How does this help me with my planning? If your answers to these questions are weak then this might not be **selective and focused** research. Choose texts that really help you make good choices.

Activity 5

Look again at this brief.

> Create a digital text providing Year 7 secondary school students with an introductory guide to your school.

1. Find and explore three different digital texts relating to this subject matter.

2. Complete a copy of the table below in as much detail as possible to record what you find.

	Choices made to suit the audience	**Choices made to achieve the purpose**	**Components and how they are used**
Text 1			
Text 2			
Text 3			

Preparing for your controlled assessment

In preparation for your controlled assessment task you should:

- Remember that you can write up to 250 words when analysing the digital texts you have researched.
- You will need to explore the techniques used in the texts to appeal to the audience.

3 Developing your proposal

When you have researched your target audience and a range of digital texts, the next step is to develop your proposal. When writing your proposal you can include up to 250 words on analysing the digital texts you have researched and another 250 words on describing your own digital text, showing how it will meet the brief.

Planning your digital text

Planning is crucial to the success of your final digital text. You need to consider the following questions:

- What content will you include?
- How will you structure it?
- What components will you need to produce or find?

Remember the scale of the text that you are creating. A short moving image text should last for about two minutes; a podcast should be about four to five minutes long; and a website should contain the home page and at least four linked pages.

Mind maps

A mind map helps you to brainstorm ideas, words and thoughts relating to a central theme or task. Producing a mind map will help you to generate ideas, structure your thoughts and make decisions.

Look at this example of a mind map for the controlled assessment task shown below. It uses colour and different shapes, which makes it easy to follow the logical sequence of ideas.

> **Create a digital text providing Year 7 secondary school students with an introductory guide to your school.**

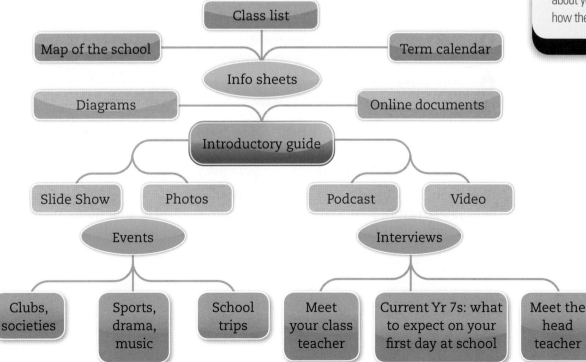

This chapter will help you to...

* plan how to structure your final product, using mind maps, concept maps, storyboards or paragraph maps

* decide what components you will include in your digital text based on the needs of your audience and purpose

* plan the gathering of the components you will need

ResultsPlus
Watch out

Visual plans are useful for sorting and communicating ideas but they are not enough on their own. The highest band of marks asks for **sustained analysis**. This means you need to write in sentences about your research and ideas, and how they informed your choices.

Look at this example of a brief:

> Create a digital text promoting a new film for teenagers.

① Produce a mind map with the purpose of the text in the centre. Group your ideas into categories.

② Decide how digital texts could be used to produce a response to this brief.

a) Divide a page into three sections with the headings 'Website or web page links', 'Audio podcast or slideshow' and 'Moving image'.

b) Group the categories from your mind map under the heading that would provide the most appropriate type of digital text.

c) Include detail – such as what you would include and whom or what you would film or record. Here's an example.

Website or web page links	Audio podcast or slideshow	Moving image
		Film review – show teenagers leaving the cinema looking excited, short interviews with two teenagers where they talk about why they enjoyed the film.
Plot – brief introduction to plot with link to character descriptions.		

③ Ask your classmates to comment on your ideas. Make notes of any feedback you receive. How could you improve your ideas?

④ Add notes from your feedback to your mind map.

Mind mapping your ideas can help you to decide which digital text is most appropriate for the brief. It will also help you to structure the content of your text and plan how to capture the components you need.

When you describe your text in your proposal, you can use mind maps to help you structure your writing. Remember to keep all of your notes, plans and background information together in an evidence folder when planning your controlled assessment task.

Storyboards

Storyboards are useful for planning the structure for moving image texts. In your storyboard you should briefly detail what will be included or said in each scene, and sketch the intended frame or captured image. Your sketches do not need to be works of art – stickmen and labels work just as well. Normally, a ten-frame storyboard would be enough to provide you with a clear structure. You can add in extra details, such as types of camera shot (see Chapter 4).

To produce a storyboard:

- divide your script into sections
- write each of the sections of script into the 'dialogue' boxes, leaving enough room to add notes about music or sound effects
- consider what images you will use, sketching them into the 'content' column
- note how long these will appear on screen
- add details about camera shots and **transitions** (these are explained in Chapter 4).

Frame/ timing	Content sketch	Detail of content, camera shot	Dialogue, sound, music	Additional notes
Frame 1: ten seconds	CINEMA FILM FILM	Establishing shot showing lots of young people leaving the cinema with posters for the film in the background.	Soundtrack of main music from the film.	First shot needs to show the excitement around seeing the film.

Activity 2

Read this script for an advertisement to promote a new hair product.

> *Do you have dull, dry, lifeless hair? Then you need Moon Silk!*
>
> *Moon Silk is the finest hair product on the market. It contains all the precious nutrients that your hair needs to make it shine, look nourished and full of body.*
>
> *Keratin and unique moisturisers blend together to make every strand of hair beautiful. The sensuous fragrance leaves your hair smelling like fresh orchids and ylang-ylang combined with aromatic mimosa and patchouli oils, to make you feel pampered and beautiful. Moon Silk for all hair types. Moon Silk, created just for you. Moon Silk – because you are …*

① Produce a storyboard showing what images could accompany each section of the script. Use between five and ten frames.

ResultsPlus
Controlled assessment tip

⚠ When producing a storyboard, draft a rough outline of your script first and then divide it into sections before deciding on the details of content, sketches and timings.

Website Extra!
A storyboard template is available on the website.

Paragraph maps

Paragraph maps are helpful for planning linear digital texts, such as podcasts. You could also use this technique to plan a voiceover for a moving image text, or for the text on individual pages of a website.

Paragraph maps help you to decide what you will include in the written text and in what order. You could write each of your ideas for paragraphs on slips of paper and then sort them into the right order. Include an introduction, followed by paragraphs on a number of separate points and finally a concluding paragraph.

A paragraph map for a podcast might start off like this:

Paragraph 1	Introduction to the subject – refer to the purpose and remember to address the audience. Grab the listener's attention by presenting the subject clearly. (Think of some background music.)
Paragraph 2	Present the first idea. Explain one of the main areas of the subject and inform/persuade/advise the audience about it.
Paragraph 3	Go on to the next area...

Planning a website

If you are going to produce a website and linked pages, you need to consider the layout. Sketch your ideas for each page and label them. Remember to include all sketches in your evidence folder. You could use other planning techniques, such as paragraph mapping, to structure your writing.

Components

Components are different elements, such as text, image and sound, which combine to make your text work. Once you have decided what type of digital text you are going to create and how you are going to structure it, you need to decide what components you want to include. Ask yourself:

• What would be suitable for the audience?

• What will achieve the purpose of the text?

In your research, you will have studied examples of existing digital texts with a similar purpose. These should have helped you to consider which components you can include to make your digital text appear professional and appeal to your audience.

Activity 3

Imagine that you have been asked to produce a digital text promoting ways in which schools and colleges could recycle more.

1. Look at the Texts A–C and Images D–F on pages 113 and 114, all of which relate to the issue of recycling. Which ones are most suitable for audiences of:

   a) adults

   b) teenagers

   c) young children?

2. For each text and each image, write a sentence explaining what makes it most suitable for the audience you have selected.

Text A *Images, logos and trademarks used with permission of WRAP © WRAP 2010*

Text B *Images, logos and trademarks used with permission of WRAP © WRAP 2010*

Text C *Images, logos and trademarks used with permission of WRAP © WRAP 2010*

Image D

Image E

Image F

You will need to create (or find) components that appeal to the specific age group of your target audience. For example, if your digital text is for a teenage audience you will need something modern and up to date to keep them interested.

You need to keep detailed notes on the research you have conducted and on which resources have been useful (or not). You will need to think about the components that have been used in existing digital texts and how you might include similar ideas in your own production. Keep a record of all of your research and thoughts; you could record them on sheets like this:

Digital Communication Unit 3: Research Record

Detail of material and where found (including web address)	Medium	Current notes	Select/Reject What ideas are useful? What could be used?

Website Extra!
A copy of this research record is available on the website.

Keeping a record

The final stage of planning is to make a detailed list of all the components that you will need to collect or capture for your digital text and how you are going to go about sourcing these. For example, if you decide to make a short film, you will need to:

- decide on locations and seek permission to use them
- arrange convenient times for filming with your teacher
- ensure that the equipment you need to use is available.

Wherever possible, plan to do your filming at your school or college as this makes the process much quicker.

- If you are producing a **moving image text** you will need to take extra footage in order to select preferred clips. Using screenshots and referring to the ones you rejected in your final evaluation will demonstrate how you have made discriminating choices.
- If you are including **still images**, make a list of all the shots you need to take, rather than wasting time taking too many pictures that will not be useful when you come to edit your text. You need to decide which types of shot will best serve the purpose.
- If you are making a **web page and associated linked pages**, you will need to decide what graphics and pictures you need to collect or capture.

No matter what type of digital text you are going to produce, keep a clear and detailed record of what you need to include.

Remind yourself of the brief in Activity 3.

1 Using a template like the one below, make a list of at least six components that you would need to use for a web page about recycling. The first has been done for you.

Component	Reason for choice of image	Where from	Notes
Photo of a landfill site or piles of rubbish.	To show how much rubbish is dumped in landfill.	Take a photo of the local landfill site or go to the nearest recycling centre.	Go at weekend to local refuse collection point. Take a few pictures so that I have enough to select the one that is best.

Writing your proposal

Your next task is to write up your proposal. In this part of your assessment you will be marked on how well you have:

- carried out relevant research which contributes to your proposal
- analysed existing digitial texts
- planned your text to meet audience needs and the brief.

Throughout this process, you will have collected a range of notes. Before you start to create your text, you need to write these up into a proposal.

Try to include the following sections in your proposal:

> an introduction – say which brief you have chosen

↓

> what you found out about your audience and purpose of the brief using research

↓

> details about any focus group work undertaken

↓

> details about what research you conducted – refer to your research record

↓

> mind maps, storyboards or paragraph maps that you have created

↓

> what components you need to gather – refer to your components list

↓

> a conclusion, stating what you hope to achieve.

Remember that you can write up to 500 words in your proposal (250 words on analysing the digital texts you have researched and 250 words on describing your own digital text).

Below are two extracts from student responses discussing their use of research.

Extract A

In order to deal with the brief, I conducted a lot of research. I looked on the Internet and found some good examples that were similar to what I was being asked to produce. I decided to use some of these ideas in my own text. For example, one of them had used pictures well.

Extract B

In order to deal with the brief, I carried out some initial research. By using Google, I typed in 'Recycling'. A wealth of websites was available to explore and the ones I looked at are recorded on my research record. I found a great deal of information on the Friends of the Earth website, www.FoE.co.uk/recycling. I liked their use of language and effective use of the triple: reduce, reuse, recycle. However, I found the home page of www.recycling-guide.co.uk more visually appealing, especially for teenagers because ...

ResultsPlus
Self assessment

When writing your proposal, make sure you:
- look at the brief carefully and select texts to explore that will help you
- explain clearly what you have learned from the texts
- explain in detail how you think you will meet the requirements of audience and purpose in your text.

Activity 5

Read the student extracts above.

1 Which extract gained higher marks? Explain your answer.

2 Make a bullet list of the key things you found out in your research. Include details of any components or design features you thought were particularly useful or helpful.

Preparing for your controlled assessment

In preparation for your controlled assessment task you should:

- Plan your digital text carefully using mind maps, storyboards or paragraph maps. Remember to think about the structure and layout of your text.

- Collect all of your notes, plans and information in an evidence folder.

- Think carefully about what components to include. Which components will be most suitable for your target audience and will achieve the purpose of the text?

- Make a list of all the components you plan to include in your digital text.

4 Capturing components

This chapter will help you to...

* gather the components that you need for your digital text, including still images, moving images, audio and written text
* seek permission to use secondary sources
* store the components you have gathered to make the editing process efficient

Key Terms

Primary source: an original piece of material – something you have created

Secondary source: something that already exists, produced by someone else

Copyright: set of rights given or granted to the author or creator of an original piece of work

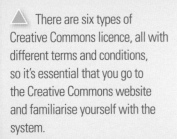

Results Plus
Controlled assessment tip

⚠ There are six types of Creative Commons licence, all with different terms and conditions, so it's essential that you go to the Creative Commons website and familiarise yourself with the system.

After you have written your proposal, the next step is to create your digital text. First you will need to capture a variety of components, such as still images, moving images, audio and written text. Remember that the components you choose will need to be appropriate for the audience and purpose of your text.

Sources and permission

In your controlled assessment task you will need to decide which components you will capture yourself (**primary sources**) and which you will take from **secondary sources**.

If you choose to use secondary sources in your digital text you must consider:

* whether you need a licence or **copyright** permission to use them
* who you need to get permission from.

Wherever possible, try to use primary sources or components created by members of your family or friends from whom you can quickly and easily seek permission. You could also use resources that are copyright-free or covered by Creative Commons licences. These can be used free of charge as long as you follow the terms of the licence and credit the original source correctly.

It is important that you list all secondary sources in your log, including those obtained from people you know.

Still images

If you are capturing your own still images you will need to plan where and how to do this.

The images below illustrate some basic camera shots you could use. These terms are used for both still and moving images.

Long shot

Mid-shot

Website Extra!
There is an information sheet about using copyright material on the website.

Extreme long shot

Close-up

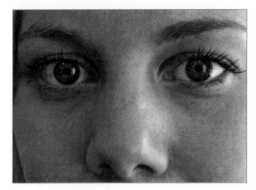

Extreme close-up

Over-the-shoulder shot

Two-shot

Three-shot

Low angle

High angle

Eye level

Website Extra!
Before completing Activity 1, you can read the information sheet on camera shots and camera angles.

Activity 1

Look at the camera shots on pages 118 and 119, and look at the information on the website about the different types of camera shot and camera angle.

1 What impact might each of the camera shots have on the audience? Complete a copy of this table.

Type of camera shot	Impact on audience
long shot	
mid-shot	
close-up	
extreme long shot	
extreme close-up	
over-the-shoulder shot	
two-shot	
three-shot	
eye level	
high angle	
low angle	

2 Look at a selection of magazines and find examples of each of these shots.

3 For each example, decide what the effect of this type of shot is on the reader and why it has been used.

4 Thinking about your digital text, note down any camera shots you might use and explain why you have chosen them.

It can be difficult and time-consuming to seek copyright permission to use existing images. If you plan your digital text carefully, you will be able to take most, if not all, of the images you require yourself.

Results**Plus**
Controlled assessment tip

△ You can collect components for your digital text in groups. Working together is a good idea because you can talk through why you are making certain choices. Make sure you always know why an image has been taken in a certain way. Make notes as you go along.

Results**Plus**
Build better answers

Look at this controlled assessment task:

Produce a digital text advising school leavers on their future choices.

■ A **Band 1** answer (1-4 marks) will capture **little** content and what is collected shows **limited understanding** of what you are meant to do.

● A **Band 3** answer (9-12 marks) will capture content with **some skill** and show **some understanding** of what is needed to fulfil the brief.

▲ An **Band 5** answer (17-20 marks) will make **adventurous and appropriate** choices when capturing content that will be handled with **imaginative skill**.

Activity 2

Imagine you are going to create a digital text providing a guide to the school for new Year 7 students. You have decided to include a range of photographs of the school in your digital text.

1. In small groups, plan which areas of the school you would like to photograph. If classrooms are to be photographed, remember to ask the teacher's permission and arrange a time that is convenient for the teacher.

2. Take a number of pictures of the same scene – maybe at slightly different angles or from various viewpoints. If your camera has a variety of functions, experiment with sepia or black and white pictures. If possible, use some special effect functions or the zoom or a wide angle shot. Become familiar with your camera and know what it can do.

3. Once you have a good collection of shots, load them onto the computer.

4. Look at your pictures in pairs or small groups. Decide:

   • which ones are most effective and why?
   • which pictures best suit the purpose and audience given in the brief?

5. Now consider what images you will need to meet the requirements of your own brief.

Remember to store your picture files carefully on a computer.

Website Extra!
Ten golden rules for making effective moving images can be found on the website. Read these rules before you go out filming!

Results**Plus**
Controlled assessment tip

 It is easy to get carried away when planning a digital video. You only have 20 hours to complete the final editing, production and collation of evidence. You need to allow an hour of editing time for every minute of footage that you film. Remember your final moving image only needs to be about three minutes long!

Results**Plus**
Watch out

■ Every selection you make is important when filming. If your video needs poor weather but it is sunny outside try to create the effect you want or film at a different time.

Moving images

Creating moving image texts is easy now that cheap camcorders, digital cameras and some mobile phones produce high-quality moving images. Most computers also have editing software as standard.

Before you go out filming, read the ten golden rules for making effective moving images on the website. You should also:

- Make sure you have all the necessary equipment. A digital camcorder or camera is recommended, as the quality of filming is good and you can zoom in and out, but it is possible to use a mobile phone, especially with the latest models, such as the iPhone, which even has built-in video editing.

- Take a spare battery, memory cards, discs and an extension lead if you are using a digital camcorder or camera.

- Use a tripod for steadier shots.

- Build a make-shift 'dolly' to move the camera without creating picture distortion or blurring. Simply attach a camera securely to an item that has wheels and ensure it runs on a smooth surface.

- Secure loose wires with tape if filming takes place in one set area and electrical equipment is being used.

Activity 3

When you go out filming, you probably won't be able to take this textbook with you.

1 Use the information that you have been given about capturing still and moving images in this chapter to produce a 'Guide to Filming and Photography' that you can refer to on location.

Activity 4

Practise some filming. Try filming a guide to your school, or make a short film providing an easy guide to filming that will reinforce the terms and techniques you have learned.

1 When filming:

- use different types of shot and the zoom facility
- try to use some close-up shots and be aware of what is happening in the background
- if anything unexpected happens, such as someone getting in the way, you will need to film the sequence again.

2 Review your filming to self-assess and identify how you can improve and perfect your technique, ready for filming your digital text. Ask yourself:

Does my film address the purpose and audience needs?

Are there any unwanted 'interruptions'?

Am I moving the camera too quickly when I **pan**?

Do I have a steady hand? (If not, consider using a tripod or mounting the camera on a trolley.)

Have I used a variety of shots? Can I name them?

Have I used any special effects?

What is good about my filming?

What needs to be improved?

Key Term

Pan: continuously moving the camera in one direction to gain a wide view or follow a moving object

Key Terms

Diegetic sound: sound that is created inside the story space/shot; usually used to emphasise realism, e.g. someone switches the radio on and we hear music

Non-diegetic sound: sound that is created outside the story space/shot; usually used to create mood or underline tension, e.g. orchestral music

Audio

Audio is an important component of many digital texts. If you are including audio in your digital text, you will need to make a range of choices, depending on the type of text that you are producing.

Diegetic sound, particularly in film-making, is sound that can be heard by the characters as well as the audience. It could include:

- sounds made by the character or objects in the clip
- voices of other characters and dialogue
- everyday sounds that naturally occur in the clip, such as sirens, cars, alarms, bells, animal noises
- music produced by characters playing an instrument or sound from a radio or other device playing in the background.

Non-diegetic sound is used to create atmosphere and mood and is not normally heard by the characters. It can be:

- music used to enhance mood and atmosphere, such as a film score
- sound effects to increase dramatic tension or effect
- a narrator, commentator or voiceover.

Activity 5

Watch a selection of TV advertisements.

1. Make a list of the different types of diegetic and non-diegetic sound used. Many advertisements use a mixture of both. An example has been provided to help you.

Advertisement	Diegetic sound	Non-diegetic sound
Compare the Market/Meerkat.com advert about explorer 'The Journey of Courageousness'	Jingle Wind Screeching birds Sea/waves Trademark 'Simples!' and squeak	Suitable stirring classical background music Narrator (Alexander)

If you produce a podcast, you will need to decide on any background sounds to enhance the spoken text.

You may choose to use a selection of sound effects, theme tunes and dialogue. There is more information on these on the companion website.

Activity 6

Website Extra!

There is an information sheet on sound effects, theme tunes and dialogue on the website. This will help you to answer Activity 6.

Watch two moving image texts (such as a news report on the *Guardian* website) and listen to two podcasts.

1 Make a list of the different uses of audio in the two types of text. Complete a copy of the table below, recording all the sounds you hear under the appropriate headings. You may need to listen to each extract two or three times to identify all the sounds.

Title	Music	Dialogue	Narrative	Other diegetic sounds	Other non-diegetic sounds

2 Using the notes in the table, answer the following questions:

a) Do the podcasts include any additional audio elements or components to those used in the moving images?

b) How does the use of sound enhance the production in each of the texts?

Recording a soundtrack

Several audio software and recording packages are available. Details of two of the main ones are provided on the companion website.

Before you start putting together your recording, gather all of your components (e.g. music or dialogue) and store them carefully.

You need to check whether:

- you have saved all the musical elements for your soundtrack
- you have recorded and saved your script
- you have saved any sound effects you wish to use.

ResultsPlus
Watch out

■ It is hard to achieve natural and effective dialogue in a digital video. You will have two problems:

- You might not have a good microphone on your camera.
- Few people can act well. Consider keeping dialogue to a minimum.

Activity 7

Find out what audio or sound editing software package is available in your school.

1 Practise using the software package available in your school or college by recording part of a prepared script.

Website Extra!

There are a number of different audio software and recording packages available. Audacity is available as a free download and is easy to use. Read the information sheet to find out more.

As well as capturing audio yourself, you may want to use audio that has been produced by someone else, such as a sound effect or music. Try to source copyright-free components for your digital text, as this is quicker and simpler.

However, if you do use a piece of audio that is covered by copyright, you must get permission to use it. Remember that most of the music that you listen to will be covered by copyright, so think carefully before deciding to use a favourite track in your digital text.

Key Term

Stereotype: showing groups of people in terms of certain widely held but oversimplified characteristics; for example, showing women as nagging housewives

Written text

Your brief will ask you to produce a digital text which communicates to a particular audience in order to achieve a specific purpose, such as informing, persuading or entertaining. You will need to use the skills that you have developed in preparation for GCSE English to help you write using an appropriate style of language.

No matter what type of digital text you are producing, the language must be appropriate for the audience and purpose. If you choose inappropriate language your text will not be successful. Try to avoid using slang and remember not to **stereotype** or include anything that could cause offence.

Activity 8

Read the following brief:

> Create a digital text promoting a new cleaning product for adults.

1 What does the brief tell you about:

a) the audience?

b) what the audience is being encouraged to do?

c) what the digital text will need to achieve?

2 Look at this extract from a draft of a script for this text. What problems can you identify in this short extract that will prevent it achieving its objectives?

> We have this new product for sale and you should try it. It is a cleaning product that will make your home sparkle. Clean and Gleam is fantastic and is available now in all supermarkets.

3 Now read the second draft of this script below.

a) What persuasive techniques (e.g. repetition, alliteration, rhetorical questions, simple sentences) does it employ?

b) If the second example were used as a voiceover, what additional components would you add to create an effective final product?

> Tired of housework? Want that perfect product that cleans everything in a flash? Then you need Clean and Gleam!
>
> Clean and Gleam removes ground-in dirt.
>
> Clean and Gleam gives you perfect results every time.

Tone and pace

Tone of voice allows the audience to judge whether the speaker is being serious or not. For example, you know based on their tone when your teacher is giving you clear instructions or when you must do as you are told.

When you are rehearsing a script for a digital text, vary the tone; when someone speaks in a monotone the production can become boring for the audience.

You should also think carefully about pace.

- Well-timed pauses can be effective in making points clear and emphasising them.
- Speeding up speech creates excitement and urgency.

Consider what would have an impact on your audience. By emphasising important points and changing speakers, your speech will have variety and be more interesting.

Activity 9

1. Write a script for a 15-second radio commercial promoting a new product of your choice.

2. Practise delivering the script, asking a partner to listen to it.

3. Share ideas about how you could edit the script to make it more persuasive and appealing. Consider these questions:

   a) Is your script imaginative and effective?

   b) Are there any other language techniques you could use to achieve your purpose?

   c) How can you vary the pace and tone of voice to convey your message?

4. Make any necessary changes to your script and present it to your classmates.

Preparing for your controlled assessment

In preparation for your controlled assessment you should:

- Decide which components you want to include in your digital text, and think about which you will capture yourself and which you will take from other sources.

- Plan how you will ensure that your still images, moving images, audio and written text are suitable for the audience and purpose.

- Make a list of all the secondary sources you want to include and check whether you need permission to use them. You will need to find out who you need to get permission from, whether you can use sources made by people you know and from whom you can easily ask permission, and whether you can use copyright-free sources or those covered by Creative Commons licences.

Website Extra!
You can use a search engine to look for Creative Commons music, moving images or still images. Visit the website to find out more about this and to explore possible components you could use.

5 Production and editing

This chapter will help you to...

* make choices about what is suitable for your audience and purpose

* make consistent choices about style

* make your digital text imaginative and effective

* make final edits to ensure your text meets the brief

Website Extra!

An information sheet on using Windows Movie Maker is available on the website.

As part of your controlled assessment task you will need to edit the content (components and features) of your digital text to make sure that it is suitable for the audience and purpose, and it is consistent, effective and meets the brief.

Remember that your planning was based on research you did about how to create an effective digital text that would meet the brief. You should refer back to these notes when producing and editing your final digital text.

Editing images

Cropping

Still images can be cropped to highlight particular features or to hide elements from the viewer. Look at the image below and then look at the image on the next page – the second image has been cropped to hide the telegraph pole and telephone lines.

Activity 1

Find an A4 image which combines a long shot with an element in the foreground, such as a view of a landscape with people closer to the camera.

1 Cut out a square in the middle of a blank A4 sheet and place it over your image in order to 'crop' different aspects of the picture.

2 What effect does cropping have on the image?

Morphing

Some software packages allow you to distort your images to create unusual, often amusing effects. This special effects software can make one image transform, or 'morph', into another. Your school may have software available to experiment with.

Making style choices

Organisations that produce texts usually have a **house style**. House style guidelines might cover language, spellings, fonts and font sizes, and the number of images to include for a particular amount of written text. The aim is that everyone who produces texts for the organisation makes the same style choices.

Key Term

House style: guidelines observed within an organisation to standardise the content and design of all its publications

Activity 2

Look at these three different news websites that are aimed at different audiences:

- **Channel 4 News**
- **ITV News**
- **BBC Newsround**

1 For each website, identify and describe the house style and what stylistic choices have been made.

2 What differences in style can you find? Explain what impact the different house styles might have on the audience of each website.

3 Why do you think it is important to maintain a specific style in a text?

ResultsPlus
Controlled assessment tip

 As you produce and edit your digital text, focus on making consistent choices so your final text looks professional. Think about creating a 'house style' that would make your text easily identifiable to your audience.

Evaluating your text so far

Take time to pause at some points during the production and editing process to evaluate the work you have done so far on your text. This means checking that what you have done successfully meets the given brief and deciding whether any changes or improvements need to be made. Ask yourself:

- What choices have I made so far to suit the audience and purpose of the text?
- What do I need to improve in order to meet the requirements of the brief?

Use the mark scheme opposite to help you evaluate your progress so far and to identify how you can improve your chances of gaining a higher mark. Remember that there are 25 marks available for how well your production meets the requirements of the brief and 20 marks for your technical skills and ability to make informed choices about the text's content.

Meeting the brief (25 marks)

Marks	Description
1-5	• basic ideas • basic editing choices made • little awareness of the purpose and audience • simple organisation
6-10	• sometimes appropriate ideas • some grasp of the purpose and audience • some editing choices made • some organisation
11-15	• ideas expressed and developed appropriately • clear sense of the purpose and audience • clear editing choices made • sound organisation with a clear structure
16-20	• ideas presented effectively • secure, sustained realisation of the purpose and audience • editing choices show consideration of the product's impact • secure organisation with a well-judged structure
17-20	• ideas are compelling and fully developed • sharply focused the purpose and audience • perceptive editing choices show consideration of the product's impact • convincing organisation with a sophisticated structure

Production and editing (20 marks)

Marks	Description
1-5	• content shows limited understanding of the brief • little content captured using digital hardware • undeveloped or repetitive content
6-10	• content shows some understanding of the brief • some content captured using digital hardware • some evidence that a range of content has been captured
11-15	• content shows clear understanding of the brief • content captured with some skill using digital hardware • evidence that a range of content has been captured
16-20	• reasoned choices made when capturing content • content captured with skill using digital hardware • evidence that a range of content has been captured for obvious effect
17-20	• adventurous and appropriate choices made when capturing content • content captured with imaginative skill using digital hardware • evidence that discriminating choices have been made when selecting content for effect

Activity 3

Website Extra!
You will need to download the mark scheme to complete Activities 3, 4 and 5.

Look at the three screenshots and student comments on pages 132 and 133. They are the first draft of a website that a student has produced in response to the following brief:

> Create a digital text promoting and informing the public about a new theme park.

1 Using the mark scheme on page 131, what marks do you think the draft website would receive? Remember that marks are awarded for meeting the requirements of the brief and for the production and editing.

Screenshot 1

The logo looks effective.

I like the font I've used and the colours show a water theme. I've made some mistakes and I think I should organise the text into paragraphs.

Home

Prices and opening times

Accommodation

Leisure and rides

Feedback

A family park was established on a site founded by the Knowles family in 1869, throughout the years the park has been many things. But 2 years ago things changed, the family was given permission to build a theme park. It has taken a full two years for the park to be completed, and cost well over £10 million to build. When the attraction was ready to open we invited the local MP (Robert Goodwill) to come and open the park. When news went out that the MP was coming to the park, the amount of people who turned out for the event was a huge success. Ever since the park opened in April this year, the amount of visitors to the park has been steadily increasing. Because of the increasing number of people turning up to the park, the money that we have been earning, we have been using to build and improve certain areas of the park. Since we have been improving certain areas we are hoping that this will give us

I have included clear and helpful links.

Screenshot 2

I've included a moving image text which I filmed on my phone. This will interest the audience.

In the future we are planning to build yet another thrilling ride, and start improving several areas of the park, such as the children's area, we really want to make it along the lines of what the park is actually about, which is of course water.
If you wish to get in touch please email us at
www.knowlesaquapark/water.com or ring 0120577837

Make sure you check out all of the website and see how good the park.

Recently we have accepted the odd party or meetings for different reasons. After a long discussion we have decided to allow for all occasions.

Reviews

"It's splashtastic!" Emma Holden – Coney Primary School

I've thought carefully about my language choices, using exciting words like 'thrilling' and pronouns to talk to the audience.

This group of children were one of the schools that had the chance to have a school trip here for the first time.

Choose a language

Portuguese
Polish
German
French
Spanish

Click here to see ways of reaching the park.

Ways of reaching the park

Catering

I've included lots of helpful information, such as contact details, directions and catering.

I've included links to translations (pretend ones) to show that I've thought about audience accessibility.

Use of photography.

'Splashtastic' is appropriate for the reviewer's age.

Screenshot 3

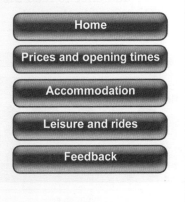

Prices & opening times

Home

Prices and opening times

Accommodation

Leisure and rides

Feedback

Ticket prices

Child – £7.99
Child under 5 – £5
Adult – £10.50
Family of 4 – £25.75

Prices

1 night – £35
2 nights – £40
3 nights – £45
4 nights – £50
5 nights – £60

If you wish to organise a party we have a choice of locations around the park, some of the areas to choose from are small and some are bigger. If you do decide to have a party at the park then it will be closed off so nobody will be able to access

The park closes from the 1st

On this page I've included details about opening times and prices.

Activity 4

Look back at the mark scheme on page 131.

1   Make notes on how the student can edit their text to improve the mark you gave them in Activity 3.

Activity 5

You will have to evaluate your own work during the controlled assessment time.

1   Look at the mark scheme on page 131 and make notes about the work you have done so far. Answer the following questions:

  a) Does your product communicate ideas clearly?

  b) Have you shown that you have edited components together effectively?

  c) Will your text successfully appeal to the intended audience and achieve its purpose?

  d) Are the organisation and structure of the text effective?

  e) What could you do to improve your text?

2   Once you have evaluated your work, write a 'to do' list and make notes about anything you now wish to change. Set yourself at least one target for something that you know you need to do better to achieve a higher mark. Make a plan for the time you have left.

Making your text imaginative and effective

Look at the screenshot of a web page below and read the comments that explain what techniques are used to make it imaginative and effective.

The designer has made the page look appealing with the use of colour and cartoon illustrations. The use of colour has not made it difficult for the audience to read the information and has been used selectively.

The tabs are clear and helpful for the audience.

Rhetorical questions make it effective because the reader knows where to locate the information they are looking for.

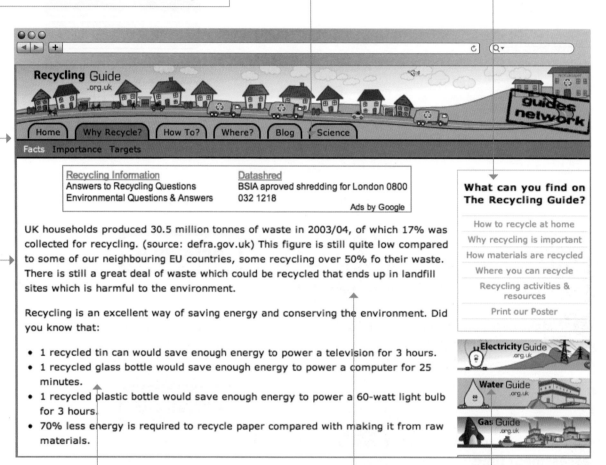

The introduction provides facts and statistics to hook the reader and generate interest.

The examples in the bullet points show the reader how easy it is to recycle and what the results of a simple action are.

This web page has original design ideas, such as cartoon houses, yet presents information in a clear and helpful way.

The whole page is easy to navigate around.

Activity 6

Look back at the initial research you carried out and compare your text with one or two of the examples of existing digital texts that you found.

1 How does your text compare to the ones you researched?

2 Is there anything you could do to make it more imaginative and effective?

Final edits

Before you complete your production, check again whether your digital text meets the brief and decide whether you need to make any final changes.

Once you have put titles, music or dialogue (if you are using them), transitions and effects into your digital text, review it to ensure that it runs smoothly and professionally. If you have used your planning time well, you will have enough time left for final amendments. If your music overruns the timing of the images, allow one of your components (or the titles or credits) to remain on screen for a few seconds longer.

Preparing for your controlled assessment

In preparation for your controlled assessment you should:

- Check that your digital text is suitable for the audience and purpose, and is consistent, effective and meets the brief.

- Practise evaluating your work on an ongoing basis. Check that the work you have completed so far meets the brief and decide whether any changes or improvements need to be made.

- If you do not have time to make all your suggested changes, concentrate on those that will help you to achieve a higher mark.

ResultsPlus
Controlled assessment tip

⚠ When editing your digital text remember to check that it meets the brief. Ask yourself these questions:

- Will it appeal to the target audience?
- Will it achieve its purpose?
- Have I organised my ideas clearly?
- Have I shown skill in combining my components?

ResultsPlus
Self assessment

When working through your controlled assessment task, check your response to make sure you have:

- presented ideas that are carried on through your editing choices
- shown that you can make editing choices that focus clearly on the intended impact
- considered the audience and purpose in every choice you make.

6 Review

This chapter will help you to...

* explain the decisions you have made, making reference to your research

* review the text you have produced, explaining the intended effects of your choices

* evaluate how effectively the product has met the brief

The final section in your controlled assessment task is the review. In your review you will need to give reasons for the choices you made in creating your digital text, drawing on feedback from others. You should refer to your initial research and explain how you selected and rejected the components to include in the final product. You can write up to 300 words in your review.

Preparing for your review

To prepare for writing your review, make notes about the final digital text that you have produced. Ask yourself these questions:

What choices or decisions did I make when producing my text?

How did I use what I learned from my research to help me make decisions?

What effect did I intend to achieve as a result of the decisions I made?

Does the product successfully meet the requirements of the brief? Is it appropriate for the target audience? Does it achieve its purpose?

Activity 1

Create a mind map to help you prepare to write your review. An example is given on page 137 to help you.

1. Write the brief you were given in the middle of a large sheet of paper.

2. Identify the key words in the brief that tell you the purpose, audience and subject matter.

3. Make notes about how you dealt with the requirements of the brief. Include comments about your research, how this fed into your planning of the text and how this can be seen in your final production.

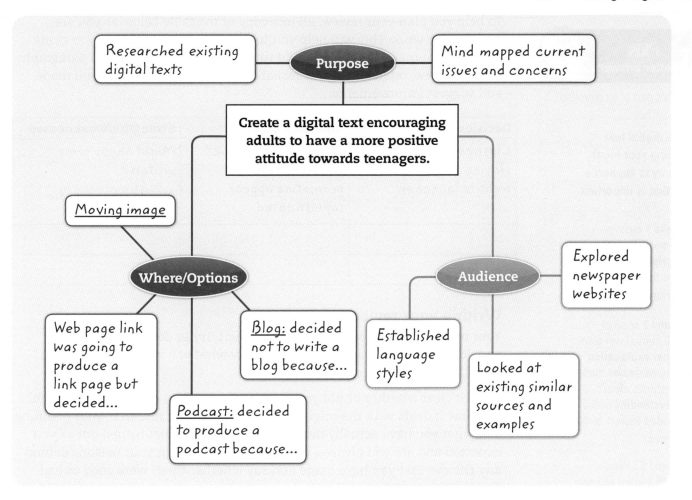

The following is the text from the mind map diagram:

Purpose
- Researched existing digital texts
- Mind mapped current issues and concerns

Create a digital text encouraging adults to have a more positive attitude towards teenagers.

Where/Options
- Moving image
- Web page link was going to produce a link page but decided...
- Podcast: decided to produce a podcast because...
- Blog: decided not to write a blog because...

Audience
- Explored newspaper websites
- Established language styles
- Looked at existing similar sources and examples

Activity 2

1. Take screenshots of your final product as evidence of what you think you have done well.

2. Label these screenshots to explain the choices you made and what effect you intended these to have on the audience.

Refer to your notes when you write up your review to help you make specific comments about your product.

You should include feedback from others about how effective your text is in your evaluation. You could ask your classmates for feedback or, if your text is aimed at a different target audience, try to get feedback from someone from the target group. Ask them to tell you what they think about your product and to suggest what you could have done to improve it. You could use a focus group for this.

To help you plan your review, fill in a copy of the table below as you are editing your work. This will help you to remember the decisions you made and why you made them. You could turn each row of notes into a paragraph in your review, referring to your research to support the choices you made and suggest improvements.

Decision	Intended impact	Strengths/weaknesses
Classical music starts playing when the website launches.	To make the product the website is promoting appear sophisticated.	Might annoy some visitors. Need to have audio turned on.

Writing your review

Your review needs to be detailed and explicit. Try to develop your points and do not assume that your teacher knew what you were doing. Explain everything you have done.

Make it clear whether or not you think that your final product is successful and how it deals with the original brief. Refer to your research, your planning and what you have actually produced. Has your product turned out as you expected and are you pleased with your work? Explain your reasons behind any choices that you have made and say whether these were good or bad decisions.

Look back at the student's Aqua Park website in Chapter 5 (pages 132–133). Below are two extracts from the student's review.

Extract 1

> _Evaluation of my Knowles' Aqua Park website_
>
> In this unit of work we were asked to: Create a digital text promoting and informing the public about a new theme park.
>
> I decided to produce my own website for a water park called Knowles' Aqua Park. Before I got on to actually creating the website, I had to conduct some research, produce rough sketches and draft out my ideas.
>
> _Purpose_
>
> The purpose of the website is to give as much information as possible. By doing this it will encourage people to visit the park, and maybe consider coming again. I think that the website met the purpose it was meant for, because it tells you everything you need to know on the website: future plans, the park's history, opening times, entrance fees, etc...

The review goes on to discuss many areas of the website, including research, planning processes and decisions made about the audience:

Extract 2

<u>Audience</u>

When I first began planning and coming up with ideas for my website, I began to make the website have a target audience for adults, but as I moved on to actually making the website, I began to realise it would be a good idea if I made the target audience for everybody. I did this because the site is easy to use, and would encourage more people to visit the park, since there is a wider range of a target audience. I also changed the target audience because I realised how easy it was to navigate around the site. I did also think of making the target audience mainly be for children since they tend to talk about new water parks and this would spread the word, but if I were to make it for everybody, it would seem more logical...

Activity 3

Read the extracts from the review.

1 How could these extracts be improved? Has the student clearly expressed their ideas?

When you are writing your review, you could include screenshots of your digital text as supporting evidence and to make sections of your text easier to understand. Screenshots are helpful for your reader and make your evaluation look professional.

Remember that you will also be marked on your writing skills, so:

- stay focused – include information and analysis that is directly relevant to your review
- structure your review carefully, grouping ideas into logical paragraphs
- use technical terms correctly
- proofread your work and check for spelling and grammatical errors.

Preparing for your controlled assessment

In preparation for your controlled assessment you should:

- Plan your review carefully to make sure it is focused on explaining the choices you made when creating your text – remember you only have up to 300 words.
- Keep a record of the decisions you make, the intended impact and the strengths and weaknesses of your decisions while you are creating and editing your text. This will make writing your review much easier.
- Remember that you will also be marked on your writing skills, so structure your review carefully and check your work for spelling and grammatical errors.

Controlled Assessment Practice

How will I be assessed?

You will be assessed under controlled conditions for this unit, which is worth 40% of your final mark. This means that you can prepare in class with your teacher and classmates, but you will have to write your response to the task and create your digital text individually in controlled conditions, without any help.

Edexcel will set the tasks that you will complete. There will be a choice of four briefs and you will choose to complete **one** brief.

You will have up to **20 hours** in controlled conditions to complete the task. You will be expected to produce a written proposal of up to **500 words,** a written review of up to **300 words** and produce a digital text. It is important that you understand what must be completed in controlled conditions and what can be done in groups both in and out of the classroom.

Section A: Proposal

- You will need to research similar texts and use this information to write a proposal for your own digital text (up to **500 words**).

- When you are doing your initial planning you can work with your teacher and classmates to develop your ideas.

- You must write your proposal individually under controlled conditions.

Section B: Communicating through your text to your audience

- You will need to produce a digital text that meets the brief and communicates its message to the target audience. You will also be assessed on your technical skill in creating your digital text.

- When you are collecting together the components (such as still images, moving images or audio) for your digital text and researching what you will need for the written text you have to produce, you can work in class with other people.

- You can also collect material together as homework.

- When you are producing and editing your text you must work individually in controlled conditions.

Section C: Reviewing your text

- You need to explain the choices you made when creating your digital text and explore audience feedback (up to **300 words**).

- You can spend time in class gathering opinions about your text; for example, by holding a focus group.

- You can prepare notes on your views about how well your text meets the brief.

- You must write your review individually in controlled conditions.

What am I being assessed on?

There are two Assessment Objectives for this unit:

A02 Analyse and evaluate how digital communication is designed to achieve effects and to engage and influence the audience – this asks you to consider how digital texts are used to impact on the audience. You will need to:

- analyse existing digital texts you have researched, exploring the techniques used to engage the audience
- explain how your text will meet the brief.

A03 Create digital communication, producing, adapting and using material to suit purpose and audience/reader – this is asking you to create a digital text to suit an audience and purpose. You will need to:

- edit the content (components and features) of your digital text in order to meet the brief
- give reasons for the choices you made in creating your text, drawing on feedback from others.

How can I succeed in this assessment?

To succeed in the assessment you need to:

✓ focus on fulfilling the brief effectively
✓ show the ideas you had when you were producing your text
✓ explain why you want to produce a text in a certain way
✓ explain the small choices you made when completing your work
✓ comment on the features and components of your digital text in the same way that you did for existing digital texts in the Unit 2 examination.

Most of your marks in this unit are for the digital text you produce. You should therefore spend time making it look professional and ensuring your ideas are imaginatively and effectively presented. Remember to stay focused on the audience and purpose, and make sure your text fulfils the brief.

Sample controlled assessment task

Instructions for the student

The task structure

What evidence should I present?

Section A Proposal

In your proposal you will

- analyse up to three of the texts you have researched, exploring the techniques used to engage audiences (up to 250 words)

- describe your own text, showing how it will meet the brief (up to 250 words).

(AO2 = 20 marks)

Section B Communicating through your text to your audience

You will edit the content (components and features) of your digital text in order to meet the brief.

(AO3 = 45 marks)

You will need to complete the Authentication and Copyright Form, which indicates where you selected sources and confirms the appropriate permissions have been given.

Section C Reviewing your text

You will give reasons for the choices you made in creating your text, drawing on feedback from others (up to 300 words).

(AO3 = 15 marks)

(Total For Task = 80 Marks)

Make sure you select texts that are similar to the brief you have chosen. Explain in your proposal what these texts tell you about what you need to do when creating your digital text.

Pay attention to the word limit. 250 words is about one side of A4 paper when you handwrite your work.

There are a lot of marks for this section. Your marker is therefore looking for a substantial piece of work. You should aim to produce a home page plus four linked pages of a website, a two–three minute long digital video or a four–five minute long podcast.

Make sure you list all the components you used from other sources. Remember to get permission to use the materials you have included in your work. It is may be easier to use components you have produced yourself than to seek permission for lots of other people's work.

It is often difficult to see the strengths and weaknesses of your own work. Seeking feedback from your classmates is a useful way of gathering notes that will help you with your review.

The tasks

You should create a digital text that fits **one** of the following briefs.

> You need to select one of the tasks. Make sure you read all the tasks before you choose the one that you want to do. Most people select the first task on any examination paper. A good way to be different and interesting might be to select a different brief.

Either

1. Create a **digital text** informing children of a recent event in the news that affects their lives.

> The audience for the digital text you have to produce will be very clear. Make sure you think carefully about what the audience needs from a text.

OR

2. Create a **digital text** encouraging teenagers to be safe in their neighbourhood.

> Notice that the brief doesn't tell you which type, or medium, of text to create. You can produce a video, podcast, website or any other type of digital text that will successfully fulfil the brief. Make sure you explain why you have selected the medium that you have in your proposal.

OR

3. Create a **digital text** promoting a product or a community service for teenagers.

> The purpose of the text will also be clear.

OR

4. Create a **digital text** helping Year 7 secondary school students to become familiar with one aspect of school life.

> The task will always be about a subject that you know about. The most successful students will look into the topic and find a way of making what they say different and interesting.

Maximise your marks

On pages 144–145 and 146–147 are some student answers to a controlled assessment task. Read the answers and examiner comments to help you understand what you need to do to gain a good mark.

Create **a digital text** informing children of a recent event in the news that affects their lives.

Student 1 – Extract typical of a grade Ⓒ answer

Proposal

This shows the student has done relevant research and analysed texts to inform the proposal – recognising the features that a young audience would need.

The CBBC website is organised on a theme of the rainforest. I think it would be a good idea to have a theme, maybe using characters that appear on a TV programme and using the website like it is their scrapbook or their doodles. I think this would work with a young audience because it wouldn't look so formal and so boring. There are lots of videos and links on the CBBC homepage too and not a lot of writing. Therefore I think I should include this on mine as it will make the site alive and interesting for the viewer.

The student has thought about the audience in their planning, but this could be a lot more detailed.

Communicating

The organisation of the text is not well judged, considering the age of the audience.

There is a range of content and it is captured clearly.

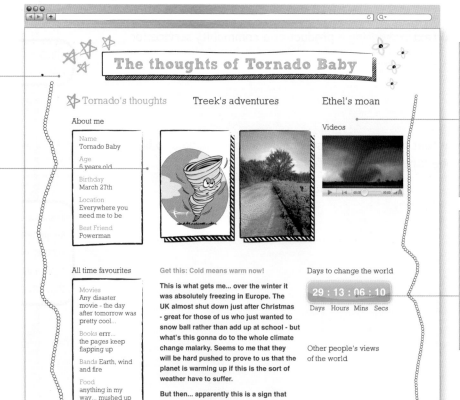

Some of the content has not been edited to work effectively on the page – for example, the images have just been dropped in and there is little sense that they have been adapted for purpose.

The audience of the page seems to be children and the page is passing on information. However, it looks complex and like it would be more accessible to teenagers.

Review

The student explains the decisions made with some link to the research they did.

I created three characters: Tornado Baby, Ethel and Treek. I thought these characters could be characters from a TV show and this is the website that links to that show — like with the CBBC website there was the linked site for Basil Brush. I thought these characters would be good for a young audience because they could treat them like teachers, sort of telling them about difficult ideas in an easy way.

They have shown they understand the effect on the audience but the level of detail here is weak and more is needed to show in-depth understanding.

Examiner summary

These parts of the answer are typical of grade C performance. The student has clearly researched and thought carefully about the audience and purpose. To improve their grade the student needs to go into a lot more detail about the intended impact of the choices that they either will make or have made. The end product shows that they have selected components but these have not been edited effectively nor does the structure help the audience.

Create **a digital text** informing children of a recent event in the news that affects their lives.

Student 2 – Extract typical of a grade Ⓐ answer

Proposal

> The CBBC website is a good example of using a simple concept to communicate difficult information. There is a rainforest theme to the page and the central window of the screen focuses on the TV programme. When you click on this link the page becomes themed on that TV programme. This sort of simplicity of navigation and layout is important for a young audience who may not be sophisticated readers. The use of bright colours and simple themes also seems important for attracting and maintaining the attention of a young audience. The rainforest theme suggests to me that I could include serious issues on my site as long as I communicate them through simple graphics and multimedia links.

The detailed analysis of the CBBC website has impacted on the proposal.

This is evidence of effective planning to meet the brief.

Communicating

The choices made when selecting content for effect are discerning. The content has also been edited to effectively work on the page.

There is excellent control of structure as the links at the top show a clear navigation around the site and the use of frames makes the page simple for the audience.

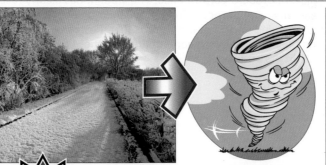

The ideas are fully developed and very effectively linked to the brief – as the whole page simply and effectively calls on the theme of a TV programme.

The image has clearly been scanned in and then edited, the photo taken and cropped. This shows effective use of hardware for obvious effect as the tornado image in particular has been edited to fit the colour theme of the page.

Review

The theme of the comic book and the close link to the television programme Comic Book Adventures mirrors the strategy used by CBBC. On this website they themed each page to one programme, so the site accompanied the events that occurred in the latest episode. As with CBBC, it was important to keep the formatting of the page simple and colourful — using minimal links and clear navigation to make sure children can access the site easily. The use of the central characters from the TV programme also serve to simplify difficult concepts, as children can link the issues to the character built up on the programme.

The choices made when selecting content for effect are discerning. The content has also been edited to work effectively on the page.

There is thorough reference to the research and how it informed the decisions made.

Examiner summary

These parts of the answer are typical of grade A performance. The student has clearly understood that they should make simple and clear choices for their audience. Therefore, although the site does not contain a range of content it does reflect the importance of simple navigation and an uncluttered structure. The choices are perceptive as the student has attempted to theme the page to the TV programme and understands that this site's purpose is to support the other medium. The simple navigation at the top showing the different pages included shows that the candidate is aware that a web page is meant to include many different media.

Glossary

Accessibility: how easy it is for the audience to find or 'access' a **digital text** (p 103)

Allusion: a reference or link to another text without actually naming that text (p 41)

Antagonist: the main villain in a film who is in conflict with the **protagonist** (p 39)

Aspiration: hope or ambition to achieve an image or lifestyle, e.g. to be popular, to have a fast car, to be seen as kind and generous (p 54)

Audience: a group of people at whom a text is aimed (p 52)

Bespoke: written or adapted for a specific user or **purpose** (p 56)

Biased representation: a **representation** that is deliberately created to influence an audience (p 37)

Blog: (web log) an online diary which provides a log of the author's thoughts, ideas, links, photos, videos or news (p 75)

Brief: a set of instructions for a task, project, investigation, etc. (p 98)

Closed question: a question where the respondent can answer with yes, no or a single word answer (p 105)

CGI (Computer Generated Imagery) animation: using computer graphics and technology in special effects (p 30)

Components: those elements that make the **digital text** work, e.g. links, home pages, icons, moving images (p 58, p 108)

Conventions: operating rules which apply in particular text types and aid audience recognition and understanding (p 60, p 106)

Copyright: a set of rights given or granted to the author or creator of an original piece of work (p 118)

Cross-genres: when at least two genres are brought together combining the conventions of both genres; for example, the superhero movie combines the genres of superhero comics and action films (p 20)

Cut: one shot ends and another begins (p 29)

Dialogue: words spoken by characters; it is scripted, rehearsed and delivered with close attention to the intended effects of the words on the viewer (p 31)

Diegetic sound: sound that is created inside the story space/shot; usually used to emphasise realism, e.g. someone switches the radio on and we hear music (p 31, p 124)

Digital text: any text that can be stored and displayed in some way using computer technology (p 5)

Digital video: a video recording that has been produced on a digital camera (or has been converted to digital) (p 67)

Fade-in: the shot begins with a black screen and gradually fades into the image (p 29)

Fade-out: the shot ends with a gradual fading of the image to a black screen (p 29)

Features: anything that relates to the presentation, layout or language of the digital text (p 53, p 58)

Focus group: a group of people who meet to discuss their views on a subject and give feedback in response to specific questions (p 105)

Genre: a type of text with certain predictable characteristics (p 18)

Genre conventions: the typical features which show the audience what genre it is (p 18)

Iconography: objects, images, characters, locations, etc. which are strongly associated with a particular genre (p 42)

Ident: like a logo, an instantly recognisable feature of a film, character or company (p 33)

Intertextual links: when one media text links or refers to another media text (p 56)

Intertextual reference: when one media text mimics or refers to another media text in a way that many consumers will recognise (p 41)

House style: guidelines observed within an organisation to standardise the content and design of all its publications (p 129)

Medium: the type of **digital text**, e.g. a **website**, **blog**, **podcast** (p 102)

Message: the intended impact, meaning or effect of the **features** and **components** (p59)

Mise-en-scène: a French phrase which means 'put in shot' (p 23)

Mobile communication: a public or private communication network which does not depend on any physical connection between those communicating (p 81)

Narrative: a story or account (p 34)

Narrative structure: the way a story is organised and shaped in terms of time and events (p 34)

Non-diegetic sound: sound that is created outside the story space/shot; usually used to create mood or underline tension, e.g. orchestral music (p 31, p 124)

Open question: a question where the respondent needs to give an extended response (p 105)

Pace: the speed at which something happens or a story develops (p 29)

Pan: (camera term) continuously moving the camera in one direction to gain a wide view or follow a moving object (p 123)

Paragraph map: a logical sequence of ideas sorted into paragraph order (p 112)

Podcast: an audio or audio-visual file which is downloaded or streamed to mobile MP3 players or personal computers (p 72)

Primary source: an original piece of material – something you have created (p 118)

Prologue: a pre-story sequence before the title credits begin (p 29)

Protagonist: the central character in a film (p 39)

Purpose: why a text has been created, e.g. to tell people what the weather will be like (p 52)

Representation: how people, places, events or ideas are shown to audiences in media texts (p 37)

Secondary source: something that already exists, produced by someone else (p 118)

Set-piece: usually a self-contained scene or sequence that stands on its own and serves as a key moment in the film (p 30)

Social network: a group of individuals or organisations connected by a common interest, friendship, belief or some other type of relationship (p 81)

Sound effect: noise that is used to create tension, to add drama or to emphasise realism, e.g. an explosion (p 31)

Stereotypes: showing groups of people in terms of certain widely held but oversimplified characteristics: for example, showing women as nagging housewives (p 37, p 126)

Storyboard: a sequence of sketches to show what will be included in each scene of a moving image text (p 111)

Sub-genre: a division of a genre. For example, romantic comedy is a sub-genre of the comedy genre (p 21)

Subversion: when a technique is used which does not fit a theory or the usual way of doing something, e.g. when a twist takes the narrative in a new direction (p 36)

Target audience: a group of people at whom a moving image text is aimed (p 20)

Transitions: how each camera shot moves into the next (p 111)

Viral marketing: a method of marketing that encourages people to pass the message to others (p 71)

Website: a collection of web pages that can be visited by anyone around the world who knows the internet address (p 64)

Wiki: a website that allows users to add and update their own content on the site. Wiki is a Hawaiian word meaning 'fast' and is often used to stand for 'What I need to Know Is' (p 57)

Published by Pearson Education Limited, a company incorporated in England and Wales, having its registered office at Edinburgh Gate, Harlow, Essex, CM20 2JE. Registered company number: 872828

Edexcel is a registered trade mark of Edexcel Limited

We would like to thank Martin Phillips for his help in the development of this material.

First published 2010

12 11 10
10 9 8 7 6 5 4 3 2 1

British Library Cataloguing in Publication Data
A catalogue record for this book is available from the British Library

ISBN 978 1 84690 710 4

Designed and typeset by Juice Creative Limited, Hertfordshire
Printed and bound in Great Britain at Scotprint, Haddington

Picture Credits
The publisher would like to thank the following for their kind permission to reproduce their photographs:

(Key: b-bottom; c-centre; l-left; r-right; t-top)

Alamy Images: Dorothea Lange / The Art Archive 59, James Boardman 5, 13, Paul Bradforth 33, Enviroman 128, 128/2, frank'n'focus 114, Wave Royalty Free 72, D. Hurst 42, Andrew Jankunas 27, Zute Lightfoot 79/2, MBI 103, NetPhotos 71, nobleIMAGES 42/3, apply pictures 42/2, CJG - Technology 5/2, 51; **Darren Phillips-Boyd:** 118l, 118r, 119/1, 119/2, 119/3, 119/4, 119/5, 119/6, 119/7, 119/8, 129l, 129c, 129r; **Mandy Esseen:** 23, 23/2; **Getty Images:** Michael Blann 113, Win Initiative 114/2, Thomas Barwick / Digital Vision 108; **Ronald Grant Archive:** 29, Dreamworks Animation 41, Warner Bros / DC Comics 30, Columbia Pictures 21, Tristar Pictures 19, Dreamworks SKG 19/2, 39, Dreamworks SKG 19/2, 39, Walt Disney Pictures / Pixar Animation Studios 35, Studio Canal / Working Title 22; **iStockphoto:** 81, 132/2, 144/3, 146/2, DSGpro 79, Lise Gagne 91, Ann Taylor-Hughes 144, 146, Matt Jeacock 82, lillisphotography 132, Daniel Loiselle 126, PippaWest 75, Chris Schmidt 5/3, 97, 121, 122, 135, Chris Schmidt 5/3, 97, 121, 122, 135, Chris Schmidt 5/3, 97, 121, 122, 135, Chris Schmidt 5/3, 97, 121, 122, 135, Eliza Snow 74, Clint Spencer 144/2; **Kobal Collection Ltd:** Warner Bros 15/2, Miramax / Barius, Claudette 38, Columbia / Rosenthal, Zade 28, 28/2, 28/3, Dreamworks Animation 69, Access Films / MTV Films / Napoleon Pictures LTD 38/2, Paramount / Gibson, Michael 25, New Line / Saul Zaentz / Wing Nut 43, Warner Bros / Legendary Pictures 43/2, Mark Johnson Productions 15, Paramount / Bad Robot 32, Columbia / Rosenthal, Zade 28, 28/2, 28/3, Columbia / Rosenthal, Zade 28, 28/2, 28/3

Cover images: *Front:* **iStockphoto; Pearson Education Ltd:** Clark Wiseman

All other images © Pearson Education

Acknowledgements
We are grateful to the following for permission to reproduce copyright material:

Figures
Figure Unit2.6.1 from cover picture for Capital FM podcast, http://itunes.apple.com/podcast/95-8-capital-fm-breakfast/id289709377, Global Radio UK; Figures Unit3.3.1, Unit3.3.2, Unit3.3.3 from Recycle Now website, http://www.recyclenow.com/schools/posters_bin_stickers/awareness_posters.html, Images, logos and trademarks used with permission of WRAP © WRAP 2010

Screenshots
Screenshot Unit2.1.1 from Sugarscape website, http://www.sugarscape.com, Hachette Filipacchi UK; Screenshot Unit2.1.2 from Screenshot of Box TV, http://www.thebox.co.uk, Channel 4; Screenshot Unit2.1.4 from http://westwood.wikispaces.com, Vicki Davis (http://coolcatteacher.blogspot.com), Teacher at Westwood Schools (www.westwoodschools.org); Screenshots Unit2.2.1, Unit2.4.2 from http://www.channel4.com; Screenshot Unit2.2.2 from http://www.oxfam.org.uk/oxfam_in_action/impact/video/behumankind_tvad_rolodex.html, reproduced with the permission of Oxfam GB, Oxfam House, John Smith Drive, Cowley, Oxford OX4 2JY, UK www.oxfam.org.uk. Oxfam GB does not necessarily endorse any text or activities that accompany the materials.; Screenshot Unit2.4.1 from WWF webpage, http://www.wwf.org.uk/joinoradopt, WWF, Photo: Black rhinoceros (Diceros bicornis) © Michel Terrettaz / WWF-Canon; Screenshot Unit2.5.2 from Boss Orange Sienna Miller advert on YouTube, http://www.youtube.com/watch?v=h9L_qgNO-LY, Proctor & Gamble (EU); Screenshot Unit2.7.2 from Telegraph blog, http://blogs.telegraph.co.uk/culture/harrymount/100044821/why-do-englishmen-dress-so-badly-in-the-heat/, copyright (c) Telegraph Media Group Limited; Screenshot Unit2.7.5 from Screenshot of Guardian Sportblog webpage http://www.guardian.co.uk/sport/blog, Copyright Guardian News & Media Ltd 2010; Screenshot Unit2CA.1 from screenshot of Don't Stop Believing, http://dontstopbelieving.five.tv, Shine Group; Screenshot Unit2CA.2 from screenshot of Twitter website, http://twitter.com © Twitter, Inc; Screenshots Unit2.2.4., Unit2.7.3. from http://imanaccounthandlergetmeoutofhere.com/, Vicky Clarfelt; Screenshot Unit3.1.1 from Moshi Monsters webpage, http://www.moshimonsters.com, Mind Candy Ltd; Screenshot Unit3.1.2 from http://www.dofe.org, Duke of Edinburgh's Award; Screenshot Unit3.5.1 from Recycling Guide webpage, http://www.recycling-guide.org.uk/facts.html, The Guides Network

Text

Extract Unit2.2.3 from Intro text, http://www.telegraph.co.uk/telegraphtv/the-cut-podcast/7838467/The-Cut-Podcast-Tim-Henman-Dizzee-Rascal-Ajami-iPhone-and-3DS.html, copyright (c) Telegraph Media Group Limited; Extract Unit2CA.3 from Guardian Music Weekly, http://www.guardian.co.uk/music/musicblog/audio/2009/dec/30/music-weekly-live-tracks, Copyright Guardian News & Media Ltd 2009; Extract Unit2.8.3 from email from British Heart Foundation; Extract Unit3.1.3 from http://www.headliners.org/storylibrary/stories/2009/leaving_it_too_late, Headliners (UK), This article was written by Charlotte Gray, 16, for Headliners, a programme of learning through journalism for young people aged 8 to 18 www.headliners.org ; Extract Unit3.2.2 from http://www.independent.co.uk/news/uk/this-britain/behind-the-stereotypes-the-shocking-truth-about-teenagers-421295.html, Robert Verkaik and Arifa Akba, The Independent 23/10/2006; Extract Unit3.2.3 from http://news.sky.com/skynews/Home/UK-News/Surgeons-Slideshow-Shock-Tactics-Help-Change-Teenagers-Attitudes-Towards-Alcohol/Article/200912315502007?lpos=UK_News_Second_UK_News_Article_Teaser_Region_0, Sky News

Websites

The websites used in this book were correct and up to date at the time of publication. It is essential for tutors to preview each website before using it in class so as to ensure that the URL is still accurate, relevant and appropriate. We suggest that tutors bookmark useful websites and consider enabling students to access them through the school/college intranet.

Disclaimer

Digital communication companion website

URL: http://www.contentextra.com/digitalcomm
Username: edexcelgcsedc
Password: DigitalComm9337

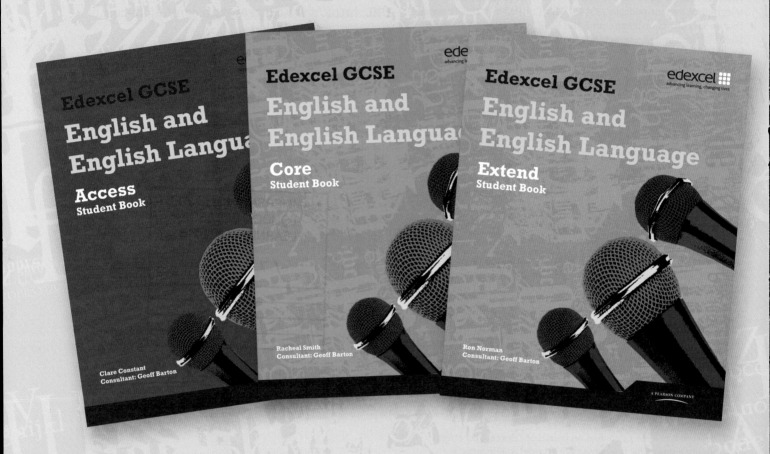